HEALTHCARE LEADERSHIP PRACTICES

How to Conquer Nursing Shortages by Improving Engagement and Retention

DR. URSULA BELL

Higgins Publishing

Dallas, Texas

Published by Higgins Publishing

www.higginspublishing.com

Higgins Publishing is committed to excellence in the publishing industry. The company reflects the philosophy established by the founder, based on Psalm 68:11,
"The Lord gave the word and great was the company of those who published it."

Book design Copyright © 2017 by Higgins Publishing. All Rights Reserved.
Cover design by Higgins Publishing

Library of Congress Control Number: 2017946219
Bell, Ursula
Healthcare Leadership Practices: How to Conquer Nursing Shortages by
Improving Engagement and Retention.

Dr. Ursula Bell – Higgins Publishing Revised Edition   November 2022
pages cm. 308 * Includes Index & References
ISBN: 978-1-941580-70-7 (PB) & ISBN: 978-1-941580-69-1 (HB)
ISBN: 978-1-941580-71-4 (EB)

1. Medical: Nursing - Management & Leadership
2. Medical: Nursing – Nursing Issues & Leadership Solutions
3. Business & Economics: Human Resources & Personnel Management

For information about special discounts for bulk purchases, subsidiary, foreign and translations rights & permissions, please contact Higgins Publishing at
sales@higginspublishing.com

Published in the United States of America

DEDICATION

To the Bells.

I am immensely grateful to my best friend and husband, Manny, and our daughters, Karen Michelle and Courtney Honor for being the rock of my life.

I could never have brought this book to fruition without your tireless support, unceasing prayers and unconditional love and support.

I love you so much.

CONTENTS

TABLE

ACKNOWLEDGMENTS

I wrote this book with significant assistance and contribution from several other people that I would like to acknowledge.

Foremost on the list are the researchers and writers from whose literature I constructed the theoretical framework of the study. They are very many and are all listed on the reference pages of this book. I was very fortunate and grateful to search, find and use highly suitable peer-reviewed literature, articles and books written by the referenced authors that immensely contributed to this writing.

Additionally, I would like to give very special thanks to Dr. Phyllis Rhodes, for her advice, prayers, encouragement, patience, and perseverance with me and my numerous questions during the several years of working on this book. Another very special note of appreciation and gratitude is for Dr. Susan Ferebee, and Dr. Regina Phelps. Dr. Ferebee provided me continuous support and constructive feedback for over five years as I researched this topic and worked progressively on the project. Dr. Phelps came to my assistance when I most needed her. As a Nurse Executive, her in-depth understanding of the topic was palpable. Her tough questions with unmatched kindness, honesty, wisdom, and her generous feedback helped me stay on target with the work at hand.

I would like to give special thanks to my friends Dr. Jade Morris, who encouraged me, lifted and kept my spirits alive when I was seemingly hopeless with the daunting process and a tedious project. Thanks to Debby Forbes, Jennifer Chernay, Dawn Parten, Carol Hasty, Hugo Garcia, Patty Eveland, and Dr. Karen Robbins for assisting in making me laugh and see light at the end of the tunnel when I appeared exasperated during the years of working on the project that culminated to this book.

Also, I wish to thank Dr. Wilmar Schaufeli and Mind Garden for authorizing me to use their surveys to conduct the research from which this work originates.

I wish to thank the Institutional Review Board (IRB) of the Medical Center of Plano (MCP, now Medical City), and the hospital's Chief Executive Officer for permitting me to use their premises to conduct the study that has provided the empirical insight shared in the book.

Recognition and gratitude are also extended to MCP's Chief Nursing Officer, and IRB coordinator. Both individuals collaborated with me diligently to ascertain the success of the project. I heartily acknowledge all the nurses of the hospital who were generous enough to dedicate time to participate honestly in the study.

Finally, a huge thank you goes to my sister Stella-Maris, and my parents for their love, amazing support, and endless prayers.

ABSTRACT

I conducted a quantitative correlational study to understand the problem that healthcare organizations face with clinical nursing workforce shortages resulting from turnover and attrition. The specific problem of the study is that a significant majority of healthcare employees indicate that they are disengaged, creating an unsafe and unhappy work environment with a high potential of being less productive and less profitable. The purpose of the study was to understand the relationships of transformational, transactional and laissez-faire leadership styles with the level of employee engagement of clinical nurses and to learn if one leadership model is a stronger predictor of clinical nurses' level of engagement.

Employee engagement behaviors include a persistent exhibition of enthusiasm, energy, and passion by employees of an organization to ensure the fulfillment of the organizational goals, believing they are trusted, and their accomplishments are valued and rewarded. I had clinical nurses in a magnet-designated acute care hospital in north Dallas, Texas in the United States complete an online survey for the study whereby they responded to questions about their leader's leadership characteristics and behaviors, and questions about the frequency of their own behaviors to engage in the organizational mission in response to their leader's leadership characteristics, practices and behaviors. The nurse participants also answered demographic questions.

The data analysis supported hypotheses that all three leadership styles are associated with clinical nurse engagement in differing ways. After reading results of the data analysis, Dr. Phelps, a respected Nurse Executive leader in a renowned acute care hospital and one of the research committee members asserted: "These results are fascinating. Very interesting."

PREFACE

The thought of sharing with the healthcare community, the study findings of this correlational research that was completed to answer the pressing question about nurse engagement and nurse leadership style is unimaginably enticing to me being a healthcare professional. After five and a half years of meticulously working on this project, Dr. Rhodes, Dr. Ferebee and Dr. Phelps curiously asked what my intent was regarding the publication of the findings of this research. Dr. Phelps stated that "the research findings are very interesting. I hope you make this publicly available to healthcare organizations of all types and to nurse leaders at every level of the leadership ladder."

My response followed "This work is very dear to me. During the course of the project, I read several books and articles on nursing, organizational culture, employee engagement, and hospital leadership. I searched for but did not find empirical evidence of a correlational study conducted between clinical nurse levels of engagement in relation to perceived nursing leadership practices. This appears to be the first one to be conducted. Adhering to the Scholars, Practitioners, and Leaders (SPL) Model, I owe it to Scholars, Practitioners, and Leaders (SPL) in healthcare, to share what was gathered from nurses at the participating hospital. Besides, for almost a decade, I collected and documented nursing perspectives on the nursing shortages, motivation, work engagement, turnover, attrition and retention in what I titled *"Voices from the Nursing Field."* My intent was to isolate themes from the "Voices" documents, leverage the findings of this research and piece both together for publishing in different readable formats. Making the findings available to all types of healthcare organizations, healthcare leaders and the nursing communities at large is of prime importance." The committee of intellectuals and scholars agreed it would be beneficial to share in adherence to the SPL model.

I sincerely hope that you will find the empirical information shared on these pages invaluable to the extent you would consciously use the recommendations to positively impact the hospital organization you lead, the nursing unit you work on, or the nursing department and team you lead or manage.

After spending a significant amount of time compiling the research data and putting this work together, I would very much like to receive feedback about what type of clinical work environments and leaders keep energies positively high at work, and what types are a de-motivator for clinical teams.

Please join me on my private discussion forum at, http://www.ursulabell.com.

CHAPTER ONE:

Prelude

"The nurses on 2 East and West are working short again today. ICU had once sick call but they can manage with their charge nurse in count till about 10am. I heard that the other units are ok for now. I have telephoned everyone on the PRN list, I called all the full-time staff to offer bonuses for picking up an extra shift, and I also called our contracted agencies. There are no nurses available to come in to help on these nursing units this morning. The East side patient-nurse ratio is 7:1. The charge nurse has two patients. There are no anticipated discharges and the census on both sides is currently 36. Last night they worked 8:1. We are also short CNAs (Certified Nurse Assistants). There are just four techs on the 2nd floor this morning. They each have nine patients. We have nine empty beds and I learned the ER is already slowly filling up. I am not sure we can accept more admissions on our units today till we find nurses to take care of these patients. It does not look bright on the side of finding more people to help today. I'll keep trying but the entire week has been like this with no floating possibilities. I just wanted to tell you before you go into discussing risk and quality in your meeting with Carra and the team this morning. Some of the potential risks you frequently discuss in relation to staffing shortages and the quality of care you often say "should be maximal without excuses" are all on the line today. Just saying."

Roseena Richards, the meticulous scheduling coordinator at a hospital where I worked several years ago, warned me as I entered the corridor leading to our offices one morning. Her words, carefully logged into "Voices from the Nursing Field" have stayed with me since then as I pondered on the possible reasons for the continual nursing shortage at the hospital, especially as I was the organization's Executive Director of quality, patient safety, and risk management.

The American nursing population is aging, and clinical nurses are confronted with a continuously challenging context in the provision of nursing care in all types of hospital environments. In 2007, Buerhaus, Auerbach, and Staiger projected the nursing shortage in America will be more than 340,000 registered nurses by 2020. And rampant attrition rates culminate in increasing shortages, creating an essential need to initiate strategies to engage and retain competent clinical nurses in health care organizations as an effort to arrest the nursing shortfall and improve quality of patient care.

While there are multiple factors that influence the engagement of hospital clinical nurses and there is not a specific predominant variable, the role of nursing leadership can fundamentally influence the clinical work environment and the engagement of nursing staff. And nursing engagement in the clinical work environment is fundamental to patient safety and the dispensation of excellent quality of patient care. The attitudes and behaviors of hospital leaders affect the behaviors, attitudes and activities of their personnel at various levels of the organization.

On the engagement spectrum, it is highly beneficial to have engaged rather than disengaged clinical nurses. Healthcare organizations with engaged, quality-driven, performance-focused, patient-centered employees obtain superior patient safety and financial results, and are better positioned to retain qualified and knowledgeable staff than those that have disengaged and unenthused personnel. Employee engagement matters significantly in service industries, especially in healthcare where errors can be catastrophic. An understanding of the significance of the distinctive input of engaged clinical nurses will enable leaders to place their great workers first as a means of enhancing the engagement of frontline, clinical nurses.

The chronic shortage of qualified nurses to provide quality patient care is exacerbated by several factors including nursing disengagement and dissatisfaction with the constantly changing work environment, and the high levels of stress, especially when working short. Although satisfied employees may behave differently from engaged staff, Job satisfaction is critical to the retention of competent clinical employees. In knowledge-based industries such as healthcare the concern for nursing staff work engagement is reasonable, and the leaders play a crucial role in assuring their engagement.

Background of the Problem

The background of the problem is that nursing is a significant provider of healthcare delivery in the United States (U.S) and all around the world. However, nurses in the U.S. health organizations are confronted with a

4

continuously challenging context of shortfall in manpower to provide safe, timely, effective, efficient patient-centered nursing care. Also, technological enhancements in medicine and the considerable reduction of inpatient hospital lengths of stay means that an increasing number of patients needing long term acute nursing care or readmission into short-term acute care hospitals for continuous care are on the rise. These patients return with the same health complaints, consequences of disease progression, or with newly diagnosed diseases, and nurses are needed to take care of them in the available hospital or clinical settings.

Additionally, the aging population in the American society also results in more elderly patients needing nursing assistance with activities of daily living. The nursing population itself is fast aging with many retirements on the horizon, and the average age of life expectancy increased dramatically in several industrialized countries since 1990. The changing features of the provision of healthcare and the patient population signify increasing demands for both quantitative and qualitative demands on nursing care. However, nursing has been experiencing a shortage in its labor force. Over the past decade, the shortfall in clinical, frontline nursing staff and the voluntary attrition of nurses has continued to be a fundamental problem affecting the delivery of safe, effective, and quality healthcare.

A study by the American Association of Colleges of Nursing (AACN) reported that by 2025, the nursing shortage will reach 260,000 Registered Nurses (RNs) with anticipated shortages of 275,215 in 2010, and 808,416 in 2020. Buerhaus, Auerbach, and Staiger projected a shortage of over 340,000 registered nurses by 2020. The AACN cited a 2007 report from the American Hospital Association explaining a registered nurse vacancy rate of 8.1% with a total of 116,000 vacant positions.

The American Nurses Association (2010) suggested that shortages are exacerbated by factors such as aging and retiring baby boomers, indicating the shortage is worsening. High patient acuity, shortened patient length of stay, deficient work environment, substandard compensation and the absence of motivation strategies further deprive healthcare facilities of competent nursing employee. The high attrition rate of nurses leaving the profession for more lucrative opportunities, the high levels of stress and burnout, a constantly changing work environment, ineffective nursing leadership styles, unfair leadership practices, inexperienced clinical leadership, and uncommitted and disengaged employees (Kleinman, 2004) further compound the nursing problems.

Leaders are fundamental for building a powerful and stable workforce in their organizations and areas of practice, and they are partially responsible for influencing employee engagement. Effective leaders do foster novel learning strategies needed to engage employees, enhance their performance, and influence organizational success. The behaviors of organizational leaders affect employee engagement on varied levels. In healthcare and in other service businesses, employee engagement drives the level of performance on certain quality metrics and the level of customer experience, satisfaction and loyalty. Without engagement, organizations find it difficult to align the efforts of their employees with the organizational goals – financial growth, optimal productivity, top branding, clientele loyalty, stakeholder safety and staff retention. As an industry that caters to the needs of the sick, afraid and fragile, healthcare requires leaders and staff who are neither disengaged nor actively disengaged, but are rather engaged. Engaged nursing employee are more likely to be passionate at their job, be less stressed, highly productive, loyal to the organization, and more thrilled with their work.

To clarify the interpretation of the term engagement, Schaufeli and Bakker (2003) indicated that "engagement is a positive, fulfilling, work-related state of mind that is characterized by vigor, dedication, and absorption" (p. 4). Engaged employees refers to workers who willingly and persistently invest in the duties of the job, manifest enthusiasm, pride, and focus in the work. Engaged employees work happily and are fully engulfed in the work (Schaufeli & Bakker, 2003).

Employees are more likely to be engaged when they have an exemplary leader who is authentic, knows and acknowledges them, is understanding and supportive, communicates openly and honestly, provides them with novel challenges, and permits them to work independently. Organizations incur high costs due to low morale of employees, lack of engagement, lack of motivation, and increased rate of absenteeism. The financial costs of these are not calculated in this study. The consequences of the actions of disengaged, low performers are monumental to organizations' bottom line. Absenteeism in nursing does not mean that the scheduled work for the absent clinical personnel does not get done. Often, it gets done at potentially higher costs and higher patient safety risks. Healthcare organizations have complex clinical settings, and clinical nurses have multiple duties, high workloads, challenging patients, administrative duties, and even committee responsibilities. When an unplanned absenteeism occurs, it makes it very difficult for all the pieces of the puzzle for the clinical work unit to align as previously anticipated.

For healthcare systems to succeed, they require clear professional and organizational rules of engagement that can assist in resolving some of nursing's issues. The rules will strengthen and replicate the positive aspects of nursing while eliminating factors that cause divisiveness in the profession, and in practice areas. For modern healthcare organizations to be prosperous, they do not only need important aspects such as financial capabilities and technological prowess but they also fundamentally require the essential human capital aka human resources. Employee engagement is an integral part of the healthcare human resources component. Hospitals need a talented frontline workforce of nurses to provide safe, timely and qualitative patient-centered care all the time to every patient. Leaders should essentially tackle the problem of clinical nurses' engagement to minimize turnover and the intent to leave, dispel employee disengagement, increase satisfaction, retention, and commitment of keen employees, increase profitability, and also meet the Institute of Medicine (IOM) recommended six aims of healthcare improvement.

Current and Systemic

The general problem considered by the research is that the healthcare industry is facing an inherent systemic shortfall in nursing labor. According to reports from the AACN, the health care industry is confronted by an imminent shortage of registered nurses with projections spanning from 275,215 in 2010 to one million registered nurses by 2025 as indicated by the DHHS, 2004. In 2009 Fox & Abrahamson shared that over ten thousand nurses have left active nursing workforce. Some of the nurses who have left nursing indicate that the major determining factors for leaving the profession include under-availability of bedside nurses, low morale, leadership concerns and lack of motivation. Needless to insist that with over ten thousand nurses' flight from the profession, turnover rate went off the roof. And turnover of hospital nurses not only contributes to nursing shortage, it has serious repercussions on the quality of patient care and the economy, and it is instrumental in the diminishing accessibility of hospital-based nursing care which remains the traditional way to provide patient care.

The specific problem is that a significant majority of healthcare clinical employees indicate that they are disengaged, which creates an unhappy work environment for themselves and their engaged counterparts, less productive and less profitable organizations (Fox, 2010) and contributes to unsafe environments of care for all hospital stakeholders. However, clinical employees in the health industry strive to stay engaged in an environment affected by several elements such as the stressfulness of the work, constant organizational change, and more significantly, nursing staff shortages. The supply of the current nurse workforce does not equate increasing demands for nursing services in the nation. According to Fox and Abrahamson, the increasing need for hospital

11

care in the nation is occurring in tandem with a significant nursing shortfall.

Employee engagement and performance are inextricably linked, which means maintaining optimal levels of staff engagement and performance is crucial to the productivity of hospitals. Therefore, clinical nurses' engagement is critical to the prosperity of healthcare organizations. Employee engagement impacts staff performance, retention, their relationship with the work to accomplish, and ultimately the organizational solvency. In a 2004 paper, Kleinman suggested that the premise of nurses' job satisfaction being a consequence of effective leadership was first advocated by Gray-Toft and Anderson in 1985. However, this research is not about the "leader is the all in all for nurses to experience job satisfaction and remain engaged." No, this is a correlational study to understand the leadership style(s) that influence the employment environment as perceived by clinical nurses, and the relationship the style has with the level of organizational engagement experienced by the nurses. Ribelin, (2003) asserted that work satisfaction is associated with leadership, and is an important aspect of clinical nurses' retention. Most people who have worked some place will concur that leader-employee relationship can significantly impact job satisfaction, morale, motivation, commitment, engagement, and the intent to leave.

Knowledge regarding work engagement for clinical nurses is finite because previous research on employee engagement was centered on managers' perspectives rather than the views of frontline nursing staff. The focus of this quantitative study was to investigate if a correlation exists between nurse managers' perceived leadership pattern and clinical nurses' organizational engagement in a major Texas hospital. Data was generated by distributing two sets of questionnaires to the nurses at the hospital.

Purposeful Endeavor

The purpose of the quantitative correlation study was to determine if a relationship exists between the perceived leadership styles of nurse managers and the level of employee engagement of clinical nurses across age and gender in a major acute care hospital in Texas. The study had two variables. The predictor variable, leadership styles of nurse managers was measured using the

Multifactor Leadership Questionnaire (MLQ), Third Edition, Form 5x-Short developed by Burns (1978) and refined by Bass and Avolio (2004).

The *Utrecht Work Engagement Scale* (UWES), also known as the Work & Well-being Survey, developed by Schaufeli and Bakker (2003) measured the criterion variable, employee engagement. The study's population included clinical nurses working at the Magnet-designated acute care hospital. The organization had 450 registered nurses during the research. The study questionnaire was sent to all the clinical nurses working in the organization who met criteria to participate in the study.

A Cause for Concern

In 2006, the American Hospital Association (AHA) reported a national shortfall of 8.5% registered nurses and the problem is on-going, and the contributing factors are diverse. Several nurses are voluntarily quitting frontline hospital work for a slew of reasons including those mentioned prior. Also, as older nurses retire and fewer nurses join the profession, a discursive sequence is developing, causing a depletion of available nurses to provide required patient care in hospitals. Although the

U.S. Department of Labor (2007) estimated a 30% job growth for registered nurses by 2014, it is alleged from research that an additional 50,000 new nurses per year is required to satisfy the demand for nurses in the workforce.

There is high social demand for nursing professionals but the nursing workforce is experiencing persistent man-power shortfall. Nurses are currently required to assume additional responsibilities to providing bedside patient-care, and in addition to their changing responsibilities, the *U.S.* is currently experiencing a growth in its aging population with more people living longer with complex and chronic ailments, causing current and future health consumers to face a situation with less human resources to provide the needed nursing care. The nursing shortage is contributing to the inadequacy of excellent customer service in healthcare, and it compromises the quality of patient care. Yes, the quality of care dispensed to patients is usually compromised in situations where nursing personnel work under-staffed because of the stressors engendered by/in such situations. And good customer service? Good customer service, which means it is not great customer

15

service – just good enough service? Well! As some hospitals in the nation report and publish their patient satisfaction scores or client experience results also known as the Hospital Consumer Assessment of Healthcare Providers and Systems (HCAPS) scores, it is important to understand that it can be challenging, if not difficult to provide great client experience when work conditions are not conducive for its provision.

To retain qualified and competent nursing employees, they need to experience Job satisfaction and feel a sense of commitment to the work environment, but there are compelling concerns for job satisfaction and organizational commitment of some professionals in knowledge-based industries such as healthcare. Health care leaders who deliberately work to prevent employees from being actively disengaged and improve their level of engagement are able to sustain high levels of morale and satisfaction, which culminate to reduced turnover and decreased costs from the consequences of turn-over.

Research data by Gallup 2009 maintained that roughly 17% of American employees were not stimulated to effectuate output. Fifty-four percent were equivocal regarding their job performance, increasing their tendency to be incorporated with unenthusiastic workers. Endres & Mancheno-Smoak confirmed that improving employee engagement and human resource productivity have become a serious agenda for human resource executives because of the high potential for those two elements to increase organizational productivity and consequently, its competitive advantage.

Conceptualizing Effective Leadership and Theories

Employees regularly embrace the idiosyncrasies of their leaders. As a profession suffering from serious staff shortfalls, healthcare organizations and clinical nursing need leaders and staff who are engaged rather than disengaged. Leadership coaching has been customarily leader-focused, and modifying the coaching so leaders recognize how they sway followers might ameliorate their understanding of how their behaviors influence the behaviors of their followers.

Healthcare is persistently evolving. Hospitals are places where policies, procedures and processes change at lightning speed, often to match the requirements of regulatory agencies, evidenced-based, and best practices.

Sustaining staff that can easily adjust and grow amidst the persistent change is a fundamental leadership objective. Employee engagement is currently one of the maxims in healthcare, and hospital leaders need to develop new strategies to engage their clinical staff because of the negative effects of nursing shortage on patient safety, patient experience/customer service, quality of care and attrition rate.

Results for engagement surveys are consistent. Globally, only approximately 21% of the workforce is engaged. In spite of the reported low workforce engagement scores, no effective strategies have been discussed, or exist for improving and sustaining staff engagement in hospitals. Engagement will result in staff loyalty, high productivity, and excitement about the work. The leadership capabilities of hospital managers have long been recognized as making important contributions to the smooth functioning of hospital units, and their leadership role is gaining increased attention in relation to their contributions to staff attitudes and their relationship to the work environment. The way that nurse managers implement their leadership roles can significantly impact the clinical work environment and the level of organizational engagement for staff nurses.

Leaders affect organizational attitudes and activities of personnel at all levels as staff look to them for example and leadership. Therefore, an improved understanding of clinical nurse engagement relative to leadership styles may provide hospital leaders with information about leadership styles and behaviors that generate a favorable response from clinical nurses, and increase their level of engagement in the organization's mission and vision. An awareness of how various leadership styles in hospital units affect staff nurse engagement may provide healthcare leaders with information that can serve to create a work environment conducive to clinical nurses' engagement.

The theoretical foundation for the study that culminated to the writing of this book was provided by leadership theory. Hospital leaders in clinical departments are facing several staff challenges which necessitate an analysis of appropriate leadership styles that can foster follower engagement.

Leadership theories have evolved through the years, departing from trait and behavioral theories to contingency and relationship theories. Since the 1920s, leaders' behaviors have significantly influenced employee performance and job satisfaction, as well as the organizational success or failure.

In the past, leadership research insisted on traits and characteristics essential for leaders managing several people, and complex organizations. Modern leadership studies are focusing on the interaction of leaders and followers, and collaboration and relationship building between them for the success of the business and organization. Through evolving leadership concepts, employee engagement remains a crucial determinant of an organization's success, and leaders assume an important role in enhancing employee performance, satisfaction, and engagement.

Leadership concepts include personality, group process, compliance, specific behaviors, influence, power and persuasion, and situation. Each leadership theory adds to the definition of leadership, and highlights the importance of organizational and employee performance. The chosen style and behaviors of leaders define their leadership effectiveness. A leader can be democratic, involving his or her employees in the decision-making process; an autocratic leader by telling employees what to do, and what will be done without consideration of employees input; or a laissez-faire/passive-avoidant leader, by leaving employees on their own without providing any direction.

Theoretical Notions of Leadership

Scholars and researchers from the pre-classical to the post-modern era have introduced, revised, and discussed several leadership theories, beginning with: (a) trait, (b) behavior, (c) contingency, (d) transformational leadership theories, (e) transactional leadership, and (f) laissez-faire/passive-avoidant leadership theories.

Trait Theory

Trait theory is the initial theory on leadership. According to the theory, the characteristics and qualities of a leader are the important factors to consider in leadership. Early leadership theorists such as Socrates and Plato indicated that leaders are born with particular traits that constitute leadership characteristics. Per the great man prince theory propounded by Machiavelli, exceptional leaders are born. Another leadership theory of the earlier era is behavior theory.

Behavior theory holds the presumption that leadership qualities are not congenital; leadership is learned, and leadership can be taught. Leadership comprises various attributes that any interested individual can learn in order to become an effective leader; hence a leader may not necessarily be born with specific traits and characteristics according to Kouzes & Posner.

Contingency Theory

Leadership contingency theory developed by Fiedler focuses on building relationships and completing tasks, without one most appropriate way to lead, added Hersey & Blanchard. In the contingency theory, environmental and situational components dictate leadership behavior. The leader's decision-making relies on the situational factors of the time, and the leader's effectiveness is determined by the performance of his or her group.

Transformational Leadership Theory

Burns proposed the transformational leadership theory. This leadership theory is known to be a process of transforming both leaders and their subordinates through high levels of collaboration. Transformational leaders engage their subordinates in a relationship that transforms both parties as individuals, and as team members of an organization.

Modern organizational structures in the new business environment should have fewer ranks of leadership that permit such collaborative efforts. Some organizations have many levels of leadership such as a president, a senior vice president, a vice president, and an assistant vice president. The supplementary levels are currently being terminated in favor of a more modern and more flat organizational structure, and work relationships are being transformed from leader and subordinate to colleagues. Avolio and Yammarino affirmed that greater flexibility to respond to more modern and changing work environments requires transformational leadership.

The transformational leadership model is highly effective in leading modern organizations, according to recent research findings. Per some researchers, the assimilation of transformational leadership style usually translates to improved client satisfaction, employee satisfaction, financial outcomes, and organizational tenure. McGuire & Kennerly indicated that transformational leaders have demonstrated that they are capable of establishing and maintaining powerful interpersonal connections with subordinates, thus improving retention and loyalty.

On the other hand, Bass and Avolio reported that transactional leadership is initiated between leaders and subordinates for the sole reason of the social exchange that is foundational to the relationship – the transaction. Transformational and transactional leadership styles are credited with increasing retention of workers and have been advanced as instrumental in helping the nursing shortage.

The leadership styles of clinical nurse leaders affect the work environment and are related to employees' job satisfaction. Although job satisfaction is a different concept from work engagement, since clinical leadership styles are said to enhance clinical nurses' job satisfaction, and retention, could it do same for staff engagement that

24

is also needed to curb the escalating shortage of nurses? Leadership theory is an indispensable and significant aspect of describing any motivational paradigm, making the theoretical framework of transformational leadership relevant and pertinent for employee engagement.

Organizational Culture and Leadership

Schein posited that organizational culture is a learned behavioral pattern that incorporates beliefs and values held by members of the organization. Organizational culture highly influences organizational activities and performance. Leaders are crucial to establishing an organization's culture, climate, structure, strategy, and the experiences of the organization's employees. Organizational culture and leadership form the dynamic that is responsible for creating a distinctive work environment as indicated by Manthey and Schein.

Researchers have noted that organizational culture is the generator of the context within which employees interpret the manners, communication styles and behaviors of others within their organization, and it helps employees to determine their compatibility or incompatibility with the work environment. Greater compatibility and credence of an organization's culture improves the likelihood of organizational engagement by its employees. Organizational culture is accountable for workers' experience in the organizational environment, and according to Jones, a strong and positive organizational culture reduces the turnover intent of talented, experienced and knowledgeable employees, discourages turnover, and enhances employee satisfaction. Healthcare organizations with modern nurse leaders are building a culture of collaboration among clinical nurses, respect for the nursing profession and each other, open, respectful, and transparent communication, a just culture, and fairness across the board with their organization. The assimilation of modern leadership styles, employee engagement, and a positive organizational culture are relevant, and may palliate nurse attrition, improve nursing job satisfaction, alleviate turnover, and potentially enhance clinical nurses' engagement.

Organizational Theory and Leadership

Organizational theory discusses and emphasizes the importance of collaborative relationships between leaders and subordinate workers currently known as colleagues to accomplish the organizational mission. Scott posited that the survival of modern organizations relies on their ability to encourage and motivate their employees to work cooperatively to accomplish the organizational objectives. As cooperate structures, organizations establish symbiotic relations with their employees, initiate opportunities for shared values, solidarity, organizational loyalty, and social integration that foster employee commitment. Scott shared that important components of organizational effectiveness include human resource management, economizing organization, authority, and informal organization. And per Scott, these components indicate the need to acknowledge that the level of employee commitment does influence organizational profits and success. And healthcare organizations need to be profitable and successful, with reduced risks of significant liability claims from preventable medical errors committed by a disengaged and stressed workforce.

As the national clinical nursing shortage persists and increased attrition of nurses continues to be rampant, a leadership style that influences the job satisfaction, commitment, and work engagement of clinical nurses is increasingly critical to healthcare organizations. Knowing and/or understanding the required and desired clinical nurse leadership style that may enhance engagement and furnish hospital leaders with concepts and strategies to retain and strengthen their workforce is critical for patient safety, quality of care and organizational success.

Understanding the Foundation

The conclusions of this book originate from a quantitative research study. A quantitative correlation study is used when a researcher seeks to relate two or more variables to determine if they influence each other and to describe and measure the level of relationship between the variables (Creswell, 2008; Leedy & Ormrod, 2010). Quantitative correlation studies analyse the relationships among variables. The objective of the research study was to examine the extent to which leadership patterns co-vary with the organizational engagement of clinical nurses.

Researchers use quantitative methods for the purpose of describing and explaining hard data. The Quantitative correlation design was used to determine the extent to which a perceived nurse leadership style covaries with the level of engagement of clinical frontline acute care nurses. Quantitative research is a research design that uses specific preformatted and validated questions to gain information from participants and apply statistical analysis to determine trends and relationships among variables. I completed this quantitative correlation study by using the Multifactor Leadership Questionnaire (MLQ) third edition, Form 5X short, by Bass and Avolio (2004), and the work engagement scale known as the Work and Well-being Survey, version 1 short (UWES) developed by Schaufeli and Bakker (2003).

The predictor variable, leadership styles was rated by clinical nurses working at the hospital where I conducted the study, using the Multifactor Leadership Questionnaire (MLQ).

The nurses measured the criterion variable, employee engagement using the work engagement scale known as the Work & Well-being Survey, version 1 short.

The MLQ is a 45-item Likert-type scale survey that rates leadership behaviors. The survey was completed by clinical nurses who were asked to identify behaviors of their clinical leaders on a range of leadership styles. The theoretical framework for the study covered a range of leadership principles that encompass transactional, transformational, and laisser-faire/passive/avoidant leadership styles in connection with the effects on work environment and organizational engagement. The clinical nurses who completed the survey based their leadership evaluation on their nurse managers and clinical leaders. Based on the perceived leadership style of the nurse manager or clinical leader, a correlation with the level of employee engagement experienced by the clinical nurses was analysed and calculated.

The Utrecht Work Engagement Scale (UWES) by Dr. Schaufeli and Mr. Bakker is a 17-item Likert-type scale survey. It was used to measure the degree of the clinical nurses' engagement at the hospital. Responses by the nurses were used to score the level of employee engagement experienced by clinical nurses in the organization. I built a demography survey that was used to analyse and understand the demographic components of the study participants. The survey for the research was administered online through a secure site. The study population included exclusively clinical nurses who worked at the hospital. Criteria for clinical nurse participation in the research included being 18 years or older, graduated from an accredited nursing school, has been employed by the organization for a minimum of three months and works on a full time, part time, and on as needed basis as a registered nurse. The nurses who participated in the study work in different clinical departments at the hospital.

Questions Worth Answering

The research questions that guided the study are as follows:

(1): Does the level of employee engagement for clinical nurses correlate with transformational leadership styles?

(2): Does the level of employee engagement for clinical nurses correlate with transactional leadership style?

(3): Does the level of employee engagement for clinical nurses correlate with laissez-faire leadership style?

The research questions were answered by identifying the leadership styles that are practiced by nurse managers, and the correlation that exists between the styles and the level of engagement in the organizational mission, experienced by clinical nurses who are 18 years of age or older. Previous research on employee engagement focused on the perspectives of leaders but not on frontline employees. I read myriad articles and books for the purpose of completing this research study, and I neither found nor came across a published research on this topic. Hence, currently from all the articles and books, there is no published research that is available on a potential correlation of perceived nurse leadership style and clinical nurses' engagement.

Some researchers have suggested that as competition on many levels increase among healthcare organizations, maintaining high levels of clinical employee engagement and performance is critical to their productivity. Engaged employees are more productive to businesses in that they easily establish and sustain excellent client service and customer relationships, and they help reduce the financial burden of employee turnover. The nursing shortage, high attrition rate, and high turnover are negatively affecting costs in healthcare organizational.

Potential and Hypothetical

Testing of the following hypotheses established the degree to which any correlation existed between nurse manager leadership style and staff engagement. The three sets of null and alternate hypotheses that addressed leadership styles and engagement levels associated with the research questions were:

H1O: No correlation exists between clinical nurses' employee engagement and transformational leadership style.

H1A: Employee engagement for clinical nurses correlates with transformational leadership style.

H2O: No correlation exists between clinical nurses' employee engagement and transactional leadership style.

HA2: Employee engagement for clinical nurses correlates with transactional leadership style.

H3O: No correlation exists between clinical nurses' employee engagement and laissez-faire leadership style.

H3A: Employee engagement for clinical nurses correlates with laissez-faire leadership style.

Piecing it Together

This section provides an explanation of the terms used in this book so each reader may have a complete understanding of the words used as I intended for them to be construed.

The Utrecht Work Engagement Scale (UWES)

The Utrecht Work Engagement Scale (UWES) by Dr. Schaufeli and Mr. Bakker measures the three elements of work engagement using a self-report 17 item Likert-type questionnaire. The three constituting components of work engagement measured by UWES are (1) vigor, (2) dedication, and (3) absorption.

Vigor is measured by self-scoring six items that relate to optimal levels of energy and resilience, the eagerness to devote effort, not being tired easily, and persistence in times of difficulties. Dedication is assessed by five items that relate to a sense of importance from one's work, feeling proud, and keenly interested in one's job, and inspired and challenged by the job (Schaufeli & Bakker). Absorption is measured using a six-item self-report that relates to being entirely consumed by one's work that time passes by unnoticeably, and detaching from the job becomes difficult (Schaufeli & Bakker). Study participants used the scale to measure employment engagement by self-scoring from a range of 0 (never), to 6 (always).

The UWES has been translated into 12 different languages and used in nine countries and varied professional and educational settings. All the scales of the UWES have demonstrated high internal consistency in several studies. The level of measurement for UWES results could be ordinal, listing the values of engagement in ranked order of vigor, dedication or absorption. To demonstrate the general level of engagement, the results of the study could also be generalized to acute care hospitals and clinical nurse settings.

The Multifactor Leadership Questionnaire (MLQ).

The Multifactor Leadership Questionnaire (MLQ) by Bass and Avolio, measures the full range leadership (FRL) model, which constitutes elements of transactional leadership, aspects of transformational leadership, and components of laisser-faire or passive/avoidant leadership. MLQ measures the FRL models using two forms namely the Leader Form and the Rater Form.

The leadership form allows leaders to rate themselves and their colleagues on the FRL behaviors. The MLQ rater form allows followers of leaders to identify where the leader stands in the range on transactional, transformational, and passive/avoidant-laissez-faire leadership behaviors. The Rater Form is the more frequently employed form to measure transactional and transformational leadership patterns (Bass & Avolio 2004) and is the form that was used for the study.

The MLQ rater form is a 5-Point Likert-type rating scale that consists of 45 survey questions to measure a continuum of leadership styles, resulting in scores. The current study employed the most recently revised version of the instrument, the Multifactor Leadership Questionnaire, Third Edition, Form 5x-short by Bass & Avolio.

The leadership elements in the FRL comprise twelve subscales. Elements in the subscale include inspirational motivation, intellectual stimulation, idealized influence (behavior and attribute), individualized consideration, contingent reward, active management-by-exception, passive management-by-exception, extra effort, effectiveness, satisfaction, and laissez-faire.

Leadership

There are several definitions of leadership. Leadership is the authority over a person or a group of individuals to pursue, and accomplish defined objectives. According to Bennis, leadership has a component of personality, behavior, action, and manners that is used in its assessment. Other criteria for analyzing leadership is the potential to build and sustain relationships, determining shared values, assumptions and performance, and financial outcomes. Leadership is the art of positively affecting others, and the aptitude of stimulating others to learn and progress toward new routes.

Leader

A leader is an individual who selects, influences, coaches, trains, mentors, and equips followers who have multiple and diverse capabilities, and inspires the followers to voluntarily and enthusiastically dispense high levels of energy to accomplish the organizational objectives and mission (Avolio & Yammarino, 2002, & 2008). A leader obtains followers' support by respectfully and clearly communicating a vision that resonates with the subordinates' beliefs and values. A leader builds coalitions and supports the empowerment of their followers, resolves complicated problems fairly and effectively, supports employees through organizational change, and motivate employees to focus their energy toward achieving success.

Transactional Leader

Bass (1990) explained that transactional leadership refers to transactions between leaders and subordinates founded on the leaders and workers establishing the requirements of the tasks to complete, and determining inherent rewards and repercussions. The transactional leader relates to subordinates only on the basis of the transaction without consideration of interpersonal relationships. The only motivation in a transactional relationship is the contract between the leader and the follower. That means you (leader) pay me (follower or subordinate) so much (my salary), and I do this much (my assigned job) for the compensation I receive. No more and no less is expected to be done in a transactional relationship. Or if less is done by the follower, there are pre-established repercussions by the leader. Notably, in a transactional leadership style, the leader and their staff or subordinates would each adhere to the terms of the contract that binds them to the organizational relationship. Period.

Laissez-faire Leadership

Bass & Riggio (2006) indicated that laissez-faire leaders postpone decision-making, avoid reaching decisive stances, and ignore the responsibilities of leadership when important matters are at stake. Bass & Avolio (1990) asserted that laissez-faire leaders are passive, avoidant, and manage-by-exception.

Employee Engagement

Employee engagement has several definitions. Employee engagement is defined as a personal sense of pride and focused energy manifested by employees in their initiative and effort to achieve the goals of an organization. Employee engagement is a persistent exhibition of enthusiasm, energy, and passion by employees to ensure the fulfillment of the organizational goals, believing they are trusted, and their accomplishments are valued and rewarded. The perceptions of trust and value give them the desire to relentlessly enhance performance, and actively contribute to the organizational success.

Employee Disengagement

Employee disengagement is the emotional and psychological detachment of employees from the work environment resulting in reduced devotion and attention to duties. While performing the duties of their jobs, several situations influence employees which result in either making them engaged or disengaged in the work environment, the organizational life, objectives, goals, and mission.

Commitment

Commitment is the power of an employee's identification with, and level of attachment to a specific organization. Employee commitment is the acceptance, and staunch trust in an organization's mission and values, the willingness to contribute a significant amount of effort to attain the organizational goals, and an unwavering desire to maintain membership of the organization (Cook, Hepworth, Wall, & Warr, 1989).

Satisfaction

Job satisfaction is a sentiment of fulfillment derived by employees from daily work experiences, activities, and relationships forged in the place of work (Harter, Schmidt, & Hayes, 2002). Employees also obtain satisfaction from knowing trust and mutual respect exists between leaders and followers (Mosadeghrad, Ferlie, & Rosenberg, 2008). Satisfaction is employees' feelings of contentment with the leader's ability to work with subordinates and colleagues, the leader's potential, and the leadership style displayed by the leader (Bass & Avolio 1995).

Retention

Retention of employees means preserving knowledgeable, productive, and valuable workers within an organization, and the avoidance of persistent turnover (Fernandez, 2007). Effective leaders in successful organizations cultivate an environment centered on attracting, recruiting, engaging, and retaining highly knowledgeable individuals (Jacob, Bond, & Galinsky, 2008). And hospital organizations need effective leaders.

Limitations

In every study, the research limitations must be revealed to avert potential issues regarding credibility of the research (Cooper & Schindler, 2003). This study was limited to one healthcare organization in North Dallas, TX. The hospital is big & has several nursing departments, and the results of the study may be generalized to other healthcare organizations around the nation.

Another limitation of this study is that while it explored possible correlations among the two variables in the study, it does not involve modifying the situation under investigation nor does it determine the cause-and-effect relationships of the variables. Although a correlation exists if, when one variable increases, the other variable either increase or decrease, "correlation alone does not in and of itself indicate causation" (Leedy & Ormrod, 2010). Therefore, the conclusions of the study though solid, are not conclusive with regards to cause-and-effect relationships.

Summary

Chapter 1 identified and discussed the concepts of nursing shortage, leadership, and engagement in the health industry. The shortage of nurses in U. S. hospitals creates multiples patient safety and quality of patient care delivery risks. The nursing profession is experiencing reduced job applicants, and several nurses have departed from active nursing workforce, citing low morale, and lack of motivation and unavailability of adequate number of bedside nurses as a major contributing factor to the unavailability of clinical nurses.

Key components of Chapter 1 included the significance of the nursing shortage to healthcare leaders, and the importance of engaging and retaining qualified clinical nurses.

In the evolving healthcare arena, as leaders focus on developing strategies to contain cost and enhance their organizational response to change, they also need to encourage the engagement of their subordinates (currently aka colleagues), by leveraging best practices in human resource management to accomplish their organizational goals. The concepts of leadership and workers' engagement are critical to organizations because focusing on excellent employees who enthusiastically devote their time to the organization is the key to success.

Understanding how leadership styles impact the level of engagement for frontline clinical nurses is important to reduce the rate of attrition in nursing, and enhance retention that is currently needed in the nursing workforce. A quantitative correlational study to determine the relationship between perceived leadership styles of nurse leaders and the degree of employee engagement that clinical nurses' experience may furnish increased awareness of the perspectives of subordinates, and help nurse leaders to initiate strategies to enhance engagement of clinical nurses in acute care hospitals.

CHAPTER TWO

Historical and Current Concepts

The goals of this book are (1) to to enlighten hospital leaders on leadership styles that foster clinical nursing engagement from nurses' perspectives, (2) contribute to the availability of scholarly literature on the topics of nursing shortage, leadership, and engagement of clinical nurses, and (3) use the results of the research to enhance strategies for increasing the engagement of clinical nurses as a means of conquering or resolving the national nursing shortages.

Below is a visual reminder of the triangular relationship that exists between hospital organizations, their leaders, and clinical employees' engagement. Each component in the triangle depends on the other, with effective organizational leaders binding workers to the organizational life, objectives, goals, mission, and culture.

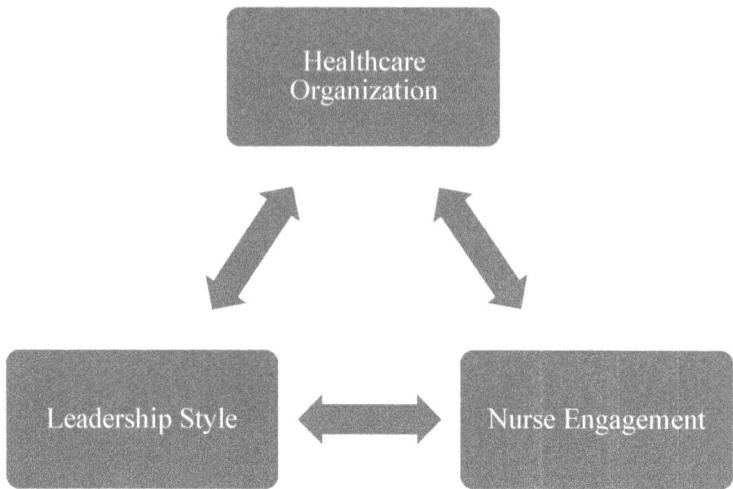

Fig.1. The relationship between hospital, leadership, and nurse engagement.

The behaviors of hospital leaders have direct impacts on the level of engagement of clinical nurses on their teams. In the context of healthcare organizations, the design of leadership has a unique influence on the attitudes of the workers. Organizational leadership style can determine the level of employee engagement, and in clinical settings, the behaviors of leaders affect the relationship of subordinates with the organization. These three components are inter-related and inseparable. Leadership behavior on one hand, and clinical nurses on the other, are both essential to the success of health care organizations. The level of organizational engagement or disengagement of clinical nurses can significantly affect the organization in various ways, and ultimately, its bottom line.

The historical overview of this book introduced in the concepts of nursing shortage, leadership, and employee engagement. For over two decades the healthcare industry in the U. S. has suffered shortages in clinical nurses and it certainly does not seem to be an easy issue to fix. However, to begin attempting to fix it at the level of individual organizations, it is important to understand certain perspectives on the issues, and why it is taking so long to resolve this issue.

Nursing Shortage

The healthcare industry in the United States is confronted by the shortage of nurses in clinical areas of work (DHHS, 2004a). Hospital organizations face challenges of quality, and continuous nursing shortfalls as a result of the nursing shortage (Elgie, 2007). Analysis of the current nursing shortfall is not new to healthcare administrators, there is no single factor contributing to the nursing shortfall (Fox & Abrahamson, 2009). However, in an environment with staff shortages and high-stress levels, leaders must develop novel and efficient strategies to motivate employees and ensure their engagement in the mission and goals of the organization is firm.

Leadership and the nursing shortage are important factors that influence the level of engagement for clinical nurses in hospitals. Analysis of the concepts of nursing shortage and leadership permits a determination of the corollary between the role of leadership, and clinical nurses' level of engagement.

Projecting the Shortage

The AACN (2008) reported that by 2025, the nursing shortage will reach 260,000 Registered Nurses (RNs), and according to a report from the Department of Health and Human Services (DHHS) (2004b), the projected nursing shortage extends through 2020. Further, the baby boomer population will consume more health-care services than former generations (DHHS, 2004b). Increased growth in technological advances may result in more preventive care and greater longevity placing new and extended demands on nurses (U.S.

Department of Labor, 2007). The aging nurse workforce is another significant contributing factor to decreasing supply. The supply of over 2.4 million registered nurses in the U. S. is almost insufficient when compared with the forecasted growth of demand (DHHS, 2004a). There are various projections of the shortage – DHHS estimated a shortage of 1 million nurses by 2020, while Buerhaus, Auerbach, & Staiger projected a shortfall of over 340,000 registered nurses by 2020. A shortage of this size would be nearly three times larger than any shortage experienced in the United States during the past ten years (Buerhaus, Auerbach & Staiger, 2007).

Despite conflicting estimations, the least estimated supply shortage poses a potential threat to the status of healthcare delivery, and is a direct threat to timely and safe delivery of patient care services. The nursing profession appears to continually suffer from manpower shortage. In 1990 hospitals in America experienced a rate of vacancy up to 11% of the nurse workforce. In 1997 the nursing shortage worsened, and by the year 2001, the AHA reported a 13% national vacancy rate of registered nurses. The nursing shortage persists, and it is part of current federal policy discussion on education.

As demands for registered nurses performing clinical practice surge and supply remains slow, hospital clinical departments continue to experience difficulties with nursing labor. And, estimations for the continual shortage in nursing human resource in the next decade may cause limited accessibility to care (Buerhaus, Auerbach, & Staiger, 2007). Researchers have identified elements such as an appealing work environment, leadership style, scheduling inventiveness, autonomy, and professional development to be attractive to nurses. There certainly is more to say about the leadership style that attracts nurses, and this research helped define some of it.

Sources of the Shortage

The staffing shortages in the nursing workforce are exacerbated by many factors including the aging of several baby boomers who have left the work force, high patient acuity, deficient work environments, coupled with substandard compensation, and the absence of motivation strategies (Fox & Abrahamson, 2009), and increasing workplace violence by patients & visitors and the risk of injury to nursing personnel.

Fox & Abrahamson (2009) indicated that government policies to assist in curbing the nursing shortage include programs such as the repayment of loan for nursing education or education debt forgiveness for graduates who work in public health after ten years of steady repayments of student loan. According to the terms of the government policy program, the federal government is responsible for the payment of 60% of the principle and interest of nursing student loan in return for a two years contract of commitment in a clinical area. The federal loan repayment program and tuition vouchers are government policies that contribute to make nursing education more accessible, affordable (Fox & Abrahamson, 2009), and encourage entry into the nursing profession in an effort to mitigate the nursing shortage.

Despite incentives such as the federal repayment assistance etcetera that have been initiated to combat and curb the nursing shortage and improve supply, demand for nurses still supersedes supply and there is indication that it might be getting worse. The nursing shortage is ongoing partially because of the shortages in available resources, but also due to admission practices in nursing programs. Between 2005 and 2006, nursing institutions denied the applications of 69,837 nursing student applicants because of the shortage in nursing instructors. The National Nursing League (2006) suggested nursing faculty vacant slots to be 1, 390. The amount of nurse instructors available was inadequate to teach the number of applicants.

Nursing education and training are no longer hospital-based. The dependence of hospitals on student nurses spending long hours in training on site while providing care to the sick no longer exists like before due to a more college and university-based nursing education (Elgie, 2007). The migration of nursing training from primarily hospital wards to universities and colleges exerts strain on emerging college-based nursing programs, which are struggling to secure sufficient number of qualified nurse instructors for the applicants.

Nursing has historically been considered a feminine profession but changing gender roles, expanded educational choices, and professional possibilities have introduced the profession to more males in recent decades. Notwithstanding, less men are willing to join the nursing workforce due to heightened diversity of career possibilities combined with stringent admission structures in registered nursing programs (Fox & Abrahamson, 2009). These factors in combination with the void in college level resources has created a system of education which is partly responsible for the shortage of registered nurses. Graduate nurses would require a growth of 90% to satisfy projected demands in 2020 (DHHS), and the number of younger nurses choosing the nursing profession as a career is inadequate to fill in the gap.

Impact on Patient Care

Several studies have determined that patient outcomes and the quality of patient care are dependent upon adequate levels of nurse staffing to patient ratio. The mortality rate of post-operative patients may increase by 7% when the increase in surgery patients case load is not proportional to nurse staffing (Aiken, Clarke, Sloan, Sochalski, & Silber, 2002). Inadequate staffing levels of clinical nurses which ensures the provision of acceptable standards of care, reduced risks of preventable patient safety occurrences, optimal quality of care and patient outcomes are in peril due to the nursing shortfall. Besides, the tendency to nurse burnout reduces with adequate staffing levels.

Mediocre compensation, the lack of respect for nurses, scheduling conflicts, and rotating shift work which contribute to low morale, are some of the key reasons advanced for the rising attrition of practicing clinical nurses. A resolution of these issues may mean that less nurses from the current practicing pool would leave the profession. And if that were the case, there would at least be a status quo in the supply of nurses but with the amplifying demand, there would still be a need to do more to prevent nursing attrition – which is contributing immensely to the shortage. Nursing shortage is partially the result of registered nurses' dissatisfaction with the functions of a nurse (Donley, 2005), and the consequences of increased turnover, reduced retention, and attrition are only secondary to the need for job satisfaction in nursing practice.

Nursing shortages coupled with dissatisfaction of nurses on the job negatively impacts patient safety and quality, and increases risks for liability because inadequate staffing levels on nursing units result in the following (1) delayed call light response time (2) delayed pager or mobile work phone response time (3) delayed calls per protocol to report critical lab values and other test results to physicians (4) delayed care and procedures as a result (5) missed physician orders (6) increased tendency and risk of making medication errors (7) decreased tendency to complete hourly patient rounds (8) Increased risk for un-witnessed and unassisted patient falls (9) decreased potential to effect two hourly patient turns per physician order or protocol (10) increased risk for patients to sustain injury from hospital acquired pressure injuries aka HAPI (11) delayed discharges (12) delayed calls to the Rapid Response Team (RRT) which leads to potential delayed interventions to safe hospitalized patients' lives (13) Increased calls for code blue since rapid response which should have been used as a proactive measure to promptly assess and treat patients' deteriorating condition was missed (14) Increased risk for patient mortality (15) increased patient and family complaints and grievances (16) Increased risk for the hospital's intangible asset –its reputation to be tarnished in the community (17) Heightened risks for unusual occurrences, adverse events, sentinel or never events (18) Increased missed opportunities to uphold guidelines for patient safety (19) Increased risk for preventable hospital-acquired infections due to haste and lack of appropriate infection prevention practices or non-compliance with policies and procedures (20) Increased risk for untimely, inefficient and nursing care (21) Increased risks of no nursing documention, incomplete documentation or false documentation with all the potential risks involved in this (22) Risk for the system to be known as highly unreliable (23) Increased risk of staff dissatisfaction, burnout, attrition, and/or riots (24)Heightened risk for licensing and accreditation issues with long lasting reputational problems (25) The list could be endless...

Healthcare environments are an essential influence in safe nursing practice. If healthcare organizations do not preserve an environment that perpetuates excellent professional practice, nursing attrition and turnover may persist, and remain a significant source of the nursing shortfall. The areas highest in clinical nurse dissatisfaction include staffing ratios and leadership behaviors. If this situation is left uncorrected nurse dissatisfaction, disengagement, attrition, and turnover will persist, compounding the shortage of the nursing workforce. Ultimately very many issues continue to result from the shortage. The most significant impacts are on patient safety and quality of patient care.

The Crisis Remains

Retaining current clinical nurses is crucial to the maintenance of the amount of practicing nurses in the workforce. Some writers have questioned the nursing shortage, but that does not take the problem away. The crisis remains an enduring issue in this nation. Lafer (2005) insisted that the scarcity of nurses is a repercussion not from inadequacy of nurses but from the unwillingness of nurses to continue working amidst work environment difficulties created by leaders. As stated earlier, per Donley (2005), the nursing shortage is the result of registered nurses' dissatisfaction with the functions of a nurse. Frontline clinical nursing is a highly challenging job. It is not easy to care for sick people, and also be obliged to sometimes clean-up after them when you have a degree and could be working at a bank, a pharmacy, an insurance office, or at the city courthouse.

According to Lafer, the number of RNs in the nation who have elected to not work in the hospital because of stagnant wages, high nurse-to-patient ratios and deteriorating working conditions is bigger than the total number of the imagined shortage. Using results from several studies as well as a 2002 survey of magnet hospitals conducted by the University of Oregon's Labor Education and Research Center, Lafer insists, "the number of working-age registered nurses who have left the profession in frustration over job conditions is significantly larger than the entire national 'shortage.'" (p. 28). Utilizing data from a survey of magnet hospitals, Lafer asserted that the healthcare industry is capable of implementing enhanced staffing levels while maintaining their economic competitiveness. The input of healthcare leaders is therefore essential in the small or big steps necessary to resolve the nursing issues.

Magnetism

The ANA (2008) reported that in 1983, the American Academy of Nurses revealed a phenomenon branded "Magnet Program" which emanated from the discourse of hospital management philosophy, leadership practices, and the quality of clinical nursing environment. The major North Dallas hospital where this study was conducted is a magnet hospital. Magnet hospitals are exemplary due to the characteristics of their leadership, and their capability to attract, recruit and retain quality professional nurses (American Nurses Association, 2008).

Research of the magnet ideal establishes leadership style as the key element in clinical nurse retention (ANA, 2008). Despite nursing shortages, hospitals with the magnet appellation report increased rates of clinical nurse retention. The model of nursing in magnet organizations inspires collaborative practices, collegial rapports with peers, and clinicians, and autonomy of nursing practice, and therefore enhances nurses' job satisfaction that may result in nurse engagement. The Magnet status is not very easy to attain. Some major and well-known hospitals have been denied the magnet status for various reasons. It is prestigious for a hospital to have magnet status, and several qualitative RNs have articulated their preference to work at Magnet-designated hospitals. The magnet status of the hospital was an important consideration for choosing to conduct this research study there.

Leadership Theories and Practices

The substantial amount of research available on leadership precludes an exhaustive review of the topic of leadership. Research on leadership spans several decades, and the concept of leadership is intricate and multi-dimensional. Provided in this section is an overview of leadership theories and styles, laying the foundation for an empirical review of the relationship between leadership styles and engagement of clinical nurses in hospitals.

The section presents a brief review of leadership theories and styles including transactional, laissez-faire, passive/avoidant, and transformational leadership, which are the leadership patterns of focus in this study.

The trait theory proposes a principle that leaders are born with idiosyncratic innate leadership traits that create the leadership skills suggesting that at birth, certain individuals are destined for leadership positions as a result of innate leadership characteristics (Bass, 1990; Boje, 2003). This is the basis for the trait theory which posits that certain individuals are formally ordained with powers to lead subordinates.

The behavior theory holds the presumption that leadership qualities are not congenital; leadership is learned, and leadership can be taught (Kouzes & Posner, 2003). Leadership comprises various attributes that any individual can learn to become an effective leader; hence a leader may not be born with specific traits (Kouzes & Posner, 2003).

The succeeding level in the expansion of the notion of leadership is the stage of recognizing the important role followers assume in the success of business organizations and enterprises. Brymer and Gray (2006) indicated that the next stage of leadership theory is leaders understanding, and acknowledging environmental signals from followers, and modifying behaviors to circumstances and situations.

Leadership theories such as the path-goal theory (Wren, 1995); the contingency theory (Fiedler, 1967), and the situational leadership theory (Hersey & Blanchard, 1982); John Maxwell (2002, 2007, 2011...) represent the evolution in expounding leadership theories.

Transformational Leadership

Burns (1978) conceptualized leadership as either transformational or transactional.

Transformational leadership theory is a leadership concept of transforming leaders and subordinates involved in the relationship. Transformational leaders empower their followers through coaching, mentoring, and training to increase their self-confidence, skills, and to encourage engagement in their tasks. Bass (1985) described transformational leaders as those who are able to develop awareness, motivation, and commitment in employees so that their approach to work effectively transcends minimum requirements, and enables subordinates to ascribe to rewards beyond personal benefits. Transformational leadership style enhances the formation of followers into leaders and fosters the achievement of the organizational vision. The leadership style aligns organizational objectives and vision with those of individual followers (Bass, 1990). Followers are crucial to the transformational relationship.

The core of transformational leadership theory is organizational structures and processes rather than particular leadership patterns (Anand, 1997). Bass (1985) asserted that transformational leadership expertise is highly relevant to competitive dynamic environments that necessitate rapid adjustments to change such as healthcare. Organizational change is an element in employee engagement, and engaged employees are more liable to welcome change than disengaged and dissatisfied personnel. This leadership theory stresses the establishment of connections between leaders and their followers.

Transformational leaders have demonstrated that they are able to effectively communicate organizational change, its vision and values, and employees' daily duties in relation to the organizational benefit (Walumba, Avolio, & Zhu, 2008). According to the transformational leadership proposition, effective leaders can achieve high results of performance that surpass expectations by advocating employees' values, self-worth, and needs at work (Gilkey, 1999). Burns (1978) indicated that leaders and their followers can accomplish higher standards of performance through motivation.

Transformational leaders incite their subordinates to accomplish shared objectives (Walumba, Avolio, &

Zhu, 2008), and they support, coach, and mentor, and give them challenging tasks to inspire their innovativeness in problem-solving. They influence their subordinates with enticing challenges and encouragement which generates understanding, importance, and expansion of the capabilities of followers (Avolio, 1999; Bass & Riggio, 2006).

Transformational leadership has a charismatic component which only partially defines the transformational leader. According to Bass and Riggio (2006), critics of the charismatic factor of transformational leaders have suggested that pseudo-transformational leaders having charisma can be dangerous, selfish, evil and destructive, and can lead followers to devastation (Bass & Riggio, 2006). Napoleon Bonaparte, Osama Bin Laden, Adolf Hitler, and Joseph Stalin are examples of charismatic leaders with destructive motivations and a lack of consideration for followers' interests (Bass & Riggio, 2006). Pseudo-transformational leaders possessing charisma are egocentric, exploitative, and are unauthentic transformational leaders (Avolio & Yammarino, 2008). This means that charisma in a leader can be viewed in a negative way. To make a point clear, transformational leaders are not necessarily charismatic leaders and may not present themselves with the charisma of a pseudo-transformational leader or a charismatic leader. However, there many great, positive charismatic leaders such as Barack Obama, Ronald Reagan and others.

Transformational leadership comprises four distinctive leadership elements: (a) idealized influence (II), (b) inspirational motivation (IM), (c) intellectual stimulation (IS), and (d) individualized consideration (IC) (Avolio & Yammarino, 2008).

Followers of transformational leaders yearn to emulate this leadership style and identify with the leader. Prior approaches to leadership focused on directives rather than participative leadership. Transformational leaders can be directive, participative, democratic or authoritarian; they may also integrate these leadership concepts (Avolio, 1999).

Transformational leaders may also be task-oriented, people-oriented or situational. Task-oriented leaders are more directive and authoritarian. People-oriented leaders are more democratic or participative. Analysts of the transformational leadership concept argue that the method is contra-democratic (Avolio, 1999; Bass

& Riggio, 2006), and depending on situational factors, transformational leaders use directive leadership principles.

During challenging situations needing immediate action, subordinates of transformational leaders may rely on the leader's idealized influence to comply when the leader enforces drastic resolutions. Subordinates consider inspirational leaders as very directive when making appeals. Intellectually stimulating leaders provide followers with challenges, while individually considerate leaders consider individual follower requirements for challenge, growth and development (Avolio, 1999; Bass & Riggio, 2006).

According to Walumba, Lawler and Avolio, (2007), the distinctive characteristics of transformational leadership are (a) idealized influence, (b) inspirational motivation, (c) intellectual stimulation, and (d) individualized consideration. Peculiar elements of transactional leadership include (a) management by exception active and, (b) contingent reward. Components of laissez-faire leadership are (a) management-by-exception passive and (b) passive-avoidance (Avolio, 1999; Bass & Riggio, 2006).

The Four Components of Transformational Leadership

Idealized Influence

Idealized Influence signifies the level of admiration followers have for the leader, when the leader's behavior attracts admiration, and inspires trust and respect. Idealized Influence is the effect of the leader's attitudes and attributes on subordinates (Bass & Riggio, 2006). Followers believe that the leader has extraordinary potential, determination, endurance, and talent, making the leader a model figure for subordinates who desire to mirror the leadership skills (Bass & Riggio, 2006). Idealized influence pertains to followers' perceptions of their leader's behavioral hallmark.

Inspirational Motivation

Inspirational motivation represents the leadership behavior that energizes and motivates followers. The leaders provide challenging opportunities for subordinates, engenders their enthusiasm, optimism, team spirit, faith in their potential & the organization, and stimulate followers to participate in envisioning a

69

fascinating future (Bass & Riggio, 2006) without undermining the current organizational realities. The leaders plainly and intelligibly articulate expectations, and exemplify commitment to objectives and shared vision (Bass & Avolio, 1995).

Intellectual Stimulation

Intellectual stimulation describes the stimulating characteristics of the leader. Leaders prompt the innovativeness and creativity of their subordinates by questioning presumptions, rephrasing problems, asking questions that make them think, and using novel strategies to approach old situations (Bass & Riggio, 2006). The Leaders encourage creative problem-solving, and novel ideas from followers, discourage public criticism of followers' errors, and involve them in problem–solving efforts. It is recommended to attempt new approaches to resolve issues, and the leaders do not censure ideas that are contrary to the leader's own perspectives (Bass & Riggio, 2006). Transformational leaders encourage followers to speak up and share their personal ideas no matter how different the ideas may be from their leader's.

Individualized Consideration

Individualized consideration alludes to the characteristic of transformational leaders who devote particular attentiveness to the individual needs of subordinates in terms of mentoring, coaching, growth and accomplishments. According to Haq, Ali, Azeem, Hijazi, Qurashi, & Quyyum, (2010) transformational leaders contribute to the growth and development of followers to superior levels of capabilities, providing them new opportunities for training in a nurturing environment. The leaders acknowledge the desires and needs of their individual subordinates, and address them individually (Bass & Riggio, 2006). Some workers need more structural work, high standards, more autonomy, and more support. The leader's behavior validates and acknowledges the significance of individual differences in terms of professional guidance (Bass & Riggio, 2006) and needs for growth and development.

Effective leaders support open communication with subordinates and perform leadership walking rounds to interact with their subordinates. Leaders listen attentively, are patient during the rounds, and show genuine interest in each employee as an individual (Bass & Riggio, 2006). In spite of the different leadership styles available, a leadership principle that incorporates the collaboration, participation, and the development of subordinates' trust positively affects employee engagement (Seijts & Crim, 2006). And enabling workers to be instrumental in making decisions for the organization encourages workers' engagement (Seijts & Crim, 2006).

Transactional Leadership Style

Transactional leadership is initiated between leaders and followers for the sole reason of the social exchange that is foundational to the relationship (Bass & Avolio, 1990; Bass & Riggio, 2006). Transactional leadership refers to transactions between leaders and subordinates, when the leaders and workers establish the duties of the tasks to complete, and then determine inherent rewards and repercussions (Bass & Riggio, 2006). In this leadership style, employees are rewarded for complying with the contract and must also anticipate punishment for non-compliance with the terms of contract. Transactional leaders use a punishment and reward style to obtain cooperation from their subordinates (Bass & Avolio, 1990).

Bass and Avolio (1990) revealed that transactional leadership relies on contingent reinforcement that can be either positive or negative contingent recompense. The negative aspects of contingent rewards are management-by-exception active (MBEA) or management-by-exception passive (MBEP). Transactional leadership blends MBEA with contingent reward (CR). MBEP is an element of passive/avoidant leadership.

Contingent reward is a beneficial agreement that persuades workers to attain high levels of growth and achievement (Bass & Avolio, 2004) for the material reward. Contingent reward can be either transactional or transformational based on the nature of the reward being psychological or material. An example of a material reward is monetary reward or salary. Psychological rewards include praise for a good job performance (Bass & Riggio, 2006).

The transactional components of contingent reward are less effective than the transformational elements. The contingent reward aspect of leadership requires leaders and subordinates to acknowledge the needs of the job to be done, and compensation provided in exchange for the successful completion of the defined duties (Bass & Riggio, 2006).

Laissez-Faire: Passive/Avoidant Leadership

According to the laissez-faire leadership theory, laissez-faire leaders postpone decision-making, are not decisive, avoid reaching decisions, and ignore the responsibilities of leadership when important matters are at stake (Bass & Riggio, 2006). Laissez-faire leaders are passive, avoidant, and manage-by-exception (Bass & Avolio, 1990; Bass & Riggio, 2006).

Passive management-by-exception refers to leaders waiting passively for subordinates to make errors before they get involved. The leader focuses on failures and corrective action to meet standards and is reactive to problems after receiving complaints (Bass & Riggio, 2006). Laissez-faire leaders are deficient in leadership capabilities. Several studies suggest laissez-faire leadership practice is the most inert and ineffective (Bass & Riggio, 2006) leadership style.

Laissez-faire leadership signifies a carefree, non-transaction-type method of leadership, whereas

74

transactional leadership is a leadership style that alludes to agreements between leaders and subordinates (Bass & Avolio, 2004). Laissez-faire leaders ignore leadership responsibilities such as taking prompt decisive actions and making decisions. They just don't know how to lead or don't lead except when something goes wrong, then they are quick to reproach.

Engagement

Employee engagement is a construct proposed in 2000 to describe commitment to work by employees (Little & Little, 2006). Writers often equate employee engagement with comparable notions such as commitment, enthusiasm, and job satisfaction (Macey & Schneider, 2008b). Varying definitions of the concept of engagement do exist, and despite the existence of several definitions of engagement, a perfect definition for engagement has not been recognized (Little & Little, 2006). Harter, Schmidt, and Hayes (2002) confirmed that interpretations of engagement include passion, enthusiasm, satisfaction, contribution to the job, and the level of energy available to accomplish the work (Schaufeli & Salanova, 2007). Additional definitions include motivation and a persistent feeling of fulfillment from the responsibilities of the job (Wildermuth & Wildermuth, 2008), new challenges, and enthusiasm (Ketter, 2008).

Employee engagement is of importance to researchers, writers, and organizational leaders (Endres & Mancheno-Smoak, 2008), and engagement has gained significant recognition in modern literature. Engagement emerged as a subject of interest when researchers indicated that the level of employee engagement is a predictor of organizational and employee outcome (Saks, 2006).

Discussions focusing on employee engagement has emerged substantially in the past four years and has been widely written in management literature and the popular press. After the introduction of the concept of engagement by the Gallup Research group, researchers and writers continued to analyze and disseminate reports indicating correlations between the engagement of workers and the success and growth of organizations. The concept of engagement has been explored by the *Washington Post*, the *Harvard Business Review, and Work Force Magazine* as well as on the websites of some human resource consulting firms. Researchers confirm that workers' engagement tremendously affects organizational efficiency and success, and leadership behavior shapes employee engagement. The relationship between leaders and subordinates affect employee engagement, and successful leadership needs the development of employee commitment and work engagement (Goffee & Jones, 2000).

Several reasons exist for investigating the level of engagement of clinical nurses. Because the notion of employee engagement is new in contemporary literature, there are limited studies about engagement by scholarly researchers (Saks, 2006). The Gallup Organization published two books on their research results on employee engagement that pointed to correlations of employee engagement and organizational profitability and staff retention (Little & Little, 2006). However, with minimal experimental verification of the efficacy of engagement on organizations, the current arguments for the effects of engagement on organizational results seem to have some empirical foundations, and necessitate further research (Saks, 2006). It is worth noting that there is no confirmation that employee engagement is an inclination or a behavior (Little & Little, 2006), or that distinguishes the rational component of engagement from the psychological aspects of engagement (Heger, 2007).

Understanding the relatively new concept of employee engagement is crucial to addressing any pertinent issue involving work engagement. Macey & Schneider have posited that academic researchers are inconsistent with interpreting the meaning of the construct of employee engagement. Little and Little stated that the term might just be a fad, an alternative to pre-existing words such as commitment, motivation or job satisfaction. This research is not about defining the construct per one group of researchers or arguing about the Gallup study because it missed highlighting and pin-pointing an in-depth definition of the term. This work utilizes the Utrecht Work Engagement Survey to determine if an association exists between the two variables in the study. Engagement is above and beyond an employee's satisfaction with an employer's arrangement, and it transcends loyalty (Macey & Schneider, 2008b). Engagement is passion and an employee's desire to expend voluntary effort for the benefit of the organization (Macey & Schneider, 2008b).

Work engagement and interrelated constructs such as job satisfaction and efficiency are novel challenges that organizational leaders should endeavor to solve (Little & Little, 2006). Some researchers have indicated that engagement is a preferred circumstance that contributes to accomplishing the goals and vision of an institution (Macey & Schneider, 2008b). The Gallup Organization (2005) and White (2008) illustrated a hurdle whereby roughly 70% of the labor force was not completely engaged. The decline in efficiency due to the absence of engagement converts into the loss of nearly $300 billion of the American aggregate national product (The Gallup Organization, 2005; LeClair & Page, 2007).

Some studies have suggested that increased staff engagement is associated with reduced turnover and attrition, and improved commitment, devotion, client satisfaction, job satisfaction, retention, and productivity. Supporting proficient workers and improving retention by building relationships that enhance engagement is a goal for several companies (Khanna, 2008). Retaining skilled and professional labor provides significant advantages such as effectiveness and competitive supremacy (Heger, 2007).

Leaders in hospital organizations need engaged and satisfied clinical employees to improve patient outcomes, quality of care, productivity, efficiency, timeliness of care, and remain relevant in the highly competitive healthcare industry.

According to Kreitner & Kinicki when company leaders consider staff engagement as an important matter and inquire about whether subordinates (a) are in symbiosis with the organization's culture, (b) are given autonomy to resolve issues, and (c) feel safe on their job, the company endures less employee attrition and turnover. Besides, workers who believe an organization pays fairly and trains adequately, experience a feeling of community and more satisfaction (Kreitner & Kinicki, 2004). Lafer (2005) asserts that healthcare management solutions to curb the nursing attrition and job dissatisfaction must include evidence-based strategies utilized by leaders of magnet hospitals to retain skilled professional nurses.

Nurse Engagement and Leadership

Leadership in healthcare is tedious and stressful, and new set of challenges surface each year for hospitals. Organizations whose leaders behave in ways that foster an engaged community easily build social capital and work within a minimally rigid and hierarchical structure (Bones, 2007). Contemporary leadership skills set include effective financial management; human resource management which includes enhancing employee effectiveness; developing relationship building skills such as trust, and nurturing employee engagement. Healthcare leaders are striving to increase worker productivity and contain costs. An advantage of staff engagement includes reduced cost secondary to decreased turnover. A plausible strategy for cost containment in hospitals is to reduce the high cost related to hospital acquired conditions, preventable medical errors from disengaged employees, disengagement and subsequent attrition.

Nursing growth will be fortified if organizations can recruit and sustain a cadre of engaged, passionate, and engrossed leaders who are confident of the future and capable of plotting a trajectory that can lead a hospital to excellence. Employees cannot be engaged unless the leader is engaged, and employees often adopt the attributes of their leaders (Kerfoot, 2008). Engaged leaders are therefore critical to securing the engagement of intrinsically motivated clinical nurses.

There's a potential for work engagement to essentially create a difference for employees, and offer organizations a competitive advantage in their industry of community. Engaged employees are positive, have a fundamental sense of zestful and effective connection to their work, and instead of considering their work to be taxing and exhausting, they consider it as challenging (Macy & Schneider, 2008b). Re-engaging disengaged staff is grueling (Fernandez, 2007) for leaders and often not worth the time. Leaders need to address the issue of employee engagement earnestly in order to help minimize the rate of staff turnover, dissuade disengagement of employees and retain committed, passionate and engaged workers.

Engaged nurses are more productive and financially beneficial to organizations. Conversely, disengaged and actively disengaged employees and high attrition cause organizations ruinous financial repercussions. Reports from the Society of Human Resource Management suggested that there are high hidden costs associated with employee turnover that negatively impact the bottom lines of organizations. The report indicated that for each employee who leaves an organization, the replacement cost is approximately one and half time (1.5 times) the employee's annual salary. Furthermore, per estimates by The American Management Association, the cost of turnover ranges anywhere from 25% to 200% of the employee's yearly compensation package.

A void in communication and ineffective communication cause reduced engagement of employees, and reduction in workers' engagement can potentially cause a rise in attrition and considerably reduce productivity. The responsibility for effective communication in an organization, employee motivation, collaboration, and organizational change rests on the shoulders of leaders (Fried & Frottler, 2008; Clawson, 2006; Yukl, 2006). Organizational change and the increase in competition make it difficult for some leaders to build effective relationships with employees. Some leaders and their subordinates are not effectively communicating, and some leaders are not providing the feedback that signifies to employees that they are cherished (Demerouti, & Bakker, 2008). Effective leaders secure numerous advantages over their competitors by not only attracting, hiring, training, motivating, and retaining skilled personnel (Fisher, Schoenfeldt, & Shaw, 2006), but also by dedicating time for open, respectful, and honest communication with employees.

Benefits of Engagement

Gallup's 2009 Employee Engagement Index (EEI) indicated that organizations with engaged employees perform better than their counterparts with disengaged employees (Gallup, 2009). According to Fox (2010), some researchers reported that in July 2008, 31% of employees were engaged, 51% were not engaged, and 17% were actively disengaged. By March 2009, 30 percent of employees were engaged, 52% were disengaged, and 18% were actively disengaged (Fox, 2010).

Researchers frequently agree that an engaged workforce is of considerable importance to outstanding performance. Engaged employees are ardent contributors to the success of an organization (Bakker, Schaufeli,

Leiter, & Taris, 2008). Research by Gallup and others affirm that engaged employees are more client-oriented, less likely to leave their employment because they are often loyal to the organization, less likely to be absent due to their intrinsic motivation, more satisfied and committed, highly productive, and more beneficial to the organization than disengaged employees.

Employee Disengagement-Consequences

Employees are categorized on a continuum from engaged, disengaged, to actively disengaged (Gallup; Fox, 2010). Engaged employees are passionate about their work, manifest a deep connection to their organization, lead innovation and help in propelling the organization upward (Fox, 2010). Actively disengaged employees are despondent at work, and sabotage the accomplishments of engaged co-workers (Fox, 2010).

Disengaged staff hold the conviction that organizational leaders consider their contributions to be insignificant. Disengaged employees concentrate on particular assignments instead of the conclusion, prefer to be directed and instructed on what to do by the managers rather than to independently resolve the issue, and seldom have a gratifying rapport with supervisors or fellow colleagues (Fox, 2010).

Employee disengagement is costly to organizations. Additional consequences of employee disengagement are reduced motivation, low level of productivity, increased absenteeism, and high levels of attrition. Several researchers have indicated that a positive social climate, good rapport with managers, supervisors and colleagues, timely performance feedback, autonomy, educational possibilities, and varied expertise are positively correlated with work engagement (Demerouti & Bakker, 2008). The Gallup Employee Engagement Index (EEI) relayed that only 33 percent of employees are engaged in their jobs, 49 percent are not engaged, and 18 percent are actively disengaged (Gallup, 2009). Basing the Employee Engagement Index on a survey of almost 42,000 randomly selected adults, Gallup researchers estimated that disengaged workers cost *U.S.* businesses $350 billion annually (Gallup, 2009).

Engagement Responsibility

In healthcare organizations, especially in hospitals, clinical staff struggles to remain engaged in an atmosphere guided by several factors from within and outside the organization. Even in well-managed healthcare organizations, it is challenging to keep the nursing workforce engaged, positive and productive (Catteeuw, Flynn, & Vonderhorst, 2007). The healthcare industry is witnessing continuous increase in innovation, technology, and demands to satisfy patients' needs (Blausten, 2009), while the supply for nurses to do the job is reducing (Buerhaus **Auerbach, & Staiger,** 2007). In spite of the myriad technological changes taking place, engaged staff want to acquire more knowledge and improve the success of the organization (Jordan, 2005).

It is worth noting that organizational leaders are not solely responsible for employee engagement. Employees are also responsible for their engagement in the work environment (Ketter, 2008). Employees are responsible for communicating their personal and common needs in the clinical environment, workplace concerns, career objectives, and satisfaction levels to leaders in order for leaders to understand the individual or collective inspirational factors of their subordinates. However, staff should contribute by providing committed efforts to the organizations they work for (Ketter, 2008). Additionally, clinical employees are responsible for nurturing their fellow colleagues and making them responsible for contributing to high standards, and quality performance (Ketter, 2008). In hospitals, it is important for clinical team members to work well together; openly communicate with, request tools for their successful performance from their leaders; and demonstrate personal responsibility and accountability for the work they willingly arrive at the organization to perform. It is difficult for the greatest and most effective leaders to motivate and inspire engagement for employees who are naturally uncommitted, professionally disconnected and actively disengaged. Employees owe it to their personal values system to dispense professional investment and dedication to the organizations that hire them, and to the systems where they leave their personal, professional footprints. It behooves clinical nurses to take pride in their professional responsibilities and the work they do, and engage in their organizational mission as dedicated partners in providing quality service to their ailing clients, their families, friends and other stakeholders of the organization. Clinical nurses' are responsible for being actively involved participants in their organization's objectives, goals and mission, live up to the expectations of their professional standards and the organization's guiding principles. Often, to achieve these requires strong, fair and engaged clinical leaders who set the pace for employees to emulate.

Employee engagement exists on various levels (Schaufeli & Bakker, 2003), that means that employees are barely totally engaged or disengaged. Some components of workers' engagement are conduct-related, while others are psychological (Macy & Schneider, 2008b). Achieving engagement can be materialized through employee recognition, and situations that inspire staff to disengage or engage. Psychological practices that control employee engagement are on a continuum of acts that they deliberately carry out, to acts that they perform inadvertently (Kahn, 1990).

Engagement and Job Satisfaction

Scholars have not concurred on a singular and best definition of work engagement, and the concept is often compared to similar notions such as job satisfaction, enthusiasm, and commitment (Macey & Schneider, 2008b). More in-depth examination of the related constructs indicate that the concepts are distinguishable, but are related (Macey & Schneider, 2008b).

Employee engagement and job satisfaction bear similarities (Little & Little, 2006). Fernandez (2007). suggested that in spite of the association of both engagement and satisfaction with organizational outcomes, engagement and satisfaction are different in that the emotional component of engagement is missing from satisfaction. Wagner (2006) asserted that there is a relationship between the level of employee engagement and the level of job satisfaction experienced by employees. However, both concepts are different. Job satisfaction does not necessarily mean employee engagement - Engaged employees are passionate about their work, perform at consistently high leves, are innovative and move their organization forward. Satisfied employees do their required jobs but not necessarily with the passion and energy of the engaged colleague. Also, satisfied employees may not be as productive as the engaged counterparts.

Nonetheless, engaged employees experience satisfaction at work, and maintain high levels of retention (Kreitner & Kinicki, 2004), but satisfied employees may still scout other employers for better opportunities, although with job satisfaction may come a certain degree of engagement. Per Wagner (2006) There is a prevailing relationship between the level of job satisfaction, and the extent of workers' engagement, and Locke (1976) submitted that work satisfaction is a psychological state attained when assessing work experience.

When leaders prevent employees from making autonomous decisions and taking initiative, they become frustrated, alienated, and feel undervalued, dissatisfied and a loss of motivation. Effective leaders support collaboration and motivation which incites satisfaction among employees (Nahavandi, 2003). Workers' behavior is commensurate with the way leadership perceives and behaves towards them(McGregor,1960). Acknowledging workers' contributions to the organization may promote satisfaction and commitment to the organization.

As indicated by Macey & Schneider, engagement is above and beyond an employee's satisfaction with an employer's arrangement, and it transcends loyalty. Engagement is passion and an employee's desire to expend voluntary effort for the benefit of the organization. Transformational and transactional styles are expected in companies where nursing job satisfaction is at its peak (McGuire & Kennerly, 2006). However, at the time of completion of this research, no leadership style has been correlated with the level of engagement for clinical nurses in acute care hospitals.

Summary

Research and literature on leadership is extensive. Chapter two explored available literature on various leadership theories and styles. Several studies have indicated correlations between leadership styles, and job satisfaction. However, despite the substantial body of literature dedicated to a variety of applications, research gaps still exist in the literature for the support of a correlation of leadership styles and clinical nurse engagement. From all the articles and books reviewed, no empirical study was found in the area of perceived leadership pattern and clinical employee engagement.

The review of the literature includes an appraisal of the writings obtainable on the topic of nursing shortage, and the concept of job satisfaction in relation to employee engagement and leadership.

The leadership approach employed by clinical leaders is indispensable to job satisfaction for clinical nurses. Additionally, leadership approach is an essential element in developing organizational commitment in nurses, but no research has measured the effects of leadership behavior on clinical nurses' engagement. Establishing a perceived nurse leadership approach from this research study identified the most appropriate leadership pattern in developing engagement for clinical nurses in acute care hospitals.

Chapter two presents a description of research data on existing literature regarding nursing shortage, perceived leadership styles, and the effects on clinical nurse engagement.

Clinical leaders are the most influential individuals in a clinical work environment for staff nurses, and transformational leadership characteristics exist most regularly in organizations presenting great degrees of nurses' job satisfaction and retention.

CHAPTER THREE:

Bringing it All to Light

This chapter provides the method and design used in the research study that culminated to this book, and it explains the appropriateness and the rationale for selecting the method and design. There are three research methodologies used to conduct sound research including qualitative methods, quantitative methods, and mixed methods (Creswell, 2005). The specific problem of research, the question, and the hypothesis determine the choice of a suitable research methodology and design (Leedy & Ormrod, 2010). The purpose of the study determines and guides the research problem, the question, and hypothesis. The purpose of the study and the question dictate the research design, procedure for data collection, and technique to analyze the data.

The quantitative method is the research method selected that was selected to conducted was the study that produced the empirical findings presented in this book. A quantitative study is a type of research in which researchers ask precise, narrow, and closed-ended questions (Creswell, 2008), collect numeric data, analyze the numbers using statistics, and coordinate the study in an impartial, unbiased manner (Leedy & Ormrod, 2010). Researchers use quantitative studies to describe trends or explain the relationship among variables (Creswell, 2005). Neuman stated that "quantitative researchers emphasize precisely measuring variables and testing hypotheses that are linked to general causal explanations" (p. 151). Neuman further argued that quantitative research entails measurement of variables, and statistical analysis of the measurement data obtained from several cases or several participants. Besides, Castellari (2010) submitted that quantitative research is useful when a researcher wishes to predict or explain the relationship between two or more variables.

Methodology Appropriateness

A researcher must consider which method and design will be most appropriate for answering the research questions, and develop a plan that leverages the selected research approach. For this study, I selected the quantitative methodology because the research questions could be answered through a regulated and logically precise method. Further, since the quantitative method allows the gathering of numerical data to explain a phenomenon (Creswell, 2008), measurement of variables, and incorporating statistical analysis to evaluate and establish hypotheses (Leedy & Ormrod, 2010). This was therefore the most appropriate approach for the study that resulted in this book as numeric data was collected representing individual perceptions of leadership style, relative frequencies that clinical nurses experienced engaged behaviors, and demographic information. The quantitative method is suited for studies in which the researcher seeks to describe or explain a phenomenon using numeric data (Creswell, 2005) such as was done in this study.

Creswell (2008) affirmed that quantitative research is the primary means for "testing objective theories by examining the relationships among variables" (p. 4). For the study from which this book is written, data was collected and quantified on leadership styles (predictor variable) of nurse managers and engagement (criterion variable) levels of nurses to determine if a relationship exist between both variables. Hence, the quantitative research methodology was the most suitable approach to accomplish the study that produced the results and recommendations used for this book results.

Rationale for Method Selection

Creswell argued that the quantitative method is suitable for a study conducted to describe or explain a phenomenon by analyzing numeric data using statistics. The quantitative researcher "conducts the inquiry in an unbiased, objective manner" (Creswell, 2005, p. 39). To complete this study, I relied on focused survey questions, recruited several participants in a major hospital, and measured the relation between the known variables by means of statistical analysis to objectively report trends, and explain the hypothesis. Creswell (2005) affirmed that a quantitative method describes or explains a phenomenon. The study was conducted to explain the relationship between variables of perceptions of leadership style and the resulting level of clinical nurses' engagement.

Sampling

Neuman (2003) indicated that probability sampling based on mathematical probability theories is normally used in quantitative research. According to Neuman, a meticulously designed and executed probability sample provides results that are equally or more accurate than attempting to reach every person in the entire population. Creswell (2005) affirmed that the probabilistic approach is the most rigorous form of sampling in quantitative research, and when the sample is representative of the population, the researcher can make generalizations to that population.

However, sometimes probability sampling is impossible in educational or social research (Creswell, 2005). Guo and Hussey argued that social science research cannot be conducted as laboratory experiments, and that study results from non-probability sampling procedures can be relevant when used concomitantly with statistical theories and interpreted appropriately.

For this study I used a non-probability sampling technique, specifically, a selective or judgment sampling strategy. Judgment sampling is a type of purposive sampling in which the researcher selects sample participants based on his judgment that the sample characterizes the population (Cooper & Schindler, 2003) to be studied. The sampling was purposive because participants had to meet specified criteria to be included in the sample. For example, they had to be registered nurses who had completed nurse training from an accredited nursing institution and been employed by the organization as clinical nurses for at least three months. Further, only nurses who provided ink signed paper informed consent, including male and female nurses from 18 years old and above participated in the study. Nurses who responded to the survey questions made up the study sample.

Sample Size

The sample size for the study was calculated using G*Power 3.0.10., a program for conducting sample size power analysis for statistical tests routinely used in social research (Faul, Erdfelder, Lang, & Buchner, 2007). The program used a priori power analysis to calculate sample size as a function of power level, significance level, and effect size.

The alternate hypotheses for the proposed study are directional. Using linear multiple regression: Fixed Model, R^2 deviation from zero, power level of .80, a small effect size ($\varrho = .15$), and alpha level of .05, a sample size of 77 participants are required. As sample size increases, power level increases (Steinberg, 2008). As illustrated below, a sample size of 118 would yield a power level of .95.

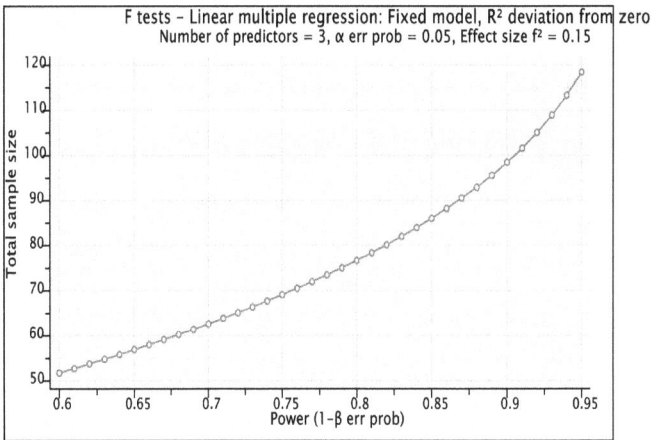

F tests – Linear multiple regression: Fixed model, R^2 deviation from zero
Number of predictors = 3, α err prob = 0.05, Effect size $f^2 = 0.15$

A Priori Sample Size Calculation by G* Power.

This figure shows how power level will increase with increasing sample size given the parameters for the study.

What Data Analysis Revealed

The study's data was analyzed and the results revealed the following. Demographic statistics from 79 usable surveys revealed that the majority of the sample's population (88%) was female and all participants (100%) were employed full times as clinical nurses in a variety of nursing departments in the organization. Participants had been in their job positions with the organization between zero and ten years. Participants were near equally split into age groups of 18 to 31: 28 participants (35%), 31 to 45: 25 participants (32%), and over 45: 25 participants (32%). A majority of the sample was female: 69 (88%), with only nine males (12%). Participants had either a BSN: 36 (46%), associate's degree: 9, (11%), or an RN 34, (43%). Twenty-seven participants (34%) had 0-5 years of service as a RN, 22 (28%) had 5-10 years of service, and 29 (37%) had over 10 years of service. A majority of the sample had been working at the organization from zero and five years: 44 (56%), while 20 (25%) reported that they had been working there over 10 years, and the remaining 14 (18%) indicated between five and ten years of working at the organization.

All 79 participants (100%) were employed full-time, and the largest proportions reported specialties in mother / baby (19, 24%), medical / surgical (16, 20%), telemetry (13, 17%), or other (13, 17%). Other participants specialized in orthopedics (3, 4%), cardiology (7, 9%), oncology (6, 8%), or operating room (1, 1%). Frequencies and percentages for the demographic data are presented in Table 3, and Figures 3 and 4 present demographic proportions.

Table 1. Frequencies and Percentages for Sample Demographic Information

Demographic	n	%
Age		
18-31	28	35
31-45	25	32
Over 45	25	32
Gender		
Female	69	88
Male	9	12
Nursing degree		
BSN	36	46

Associates	9	11
RN	34	43
Total years of service as a Registered Nurse		
0-5 years	27	34
5-10 years	22	28
Over 10 years	29	37
Total years of service as an RN in current hospital		
0-5 years	44	56
5-10 years	14	18
Over 10 years	20	25
Employee type		
Full time	79	100
Part time	0	0
Per diem	0	0
Nursing specialty		
Medical / surgical	16	20
Orthopedics	3	4
Cardiology	7	9
Oncology	6	8
Telemetry	13	17
OR	1	1
Mother / baby	19	24
Other	13	17

Note. Due to rounding error, some percentages may not sum to 100%.

Gender

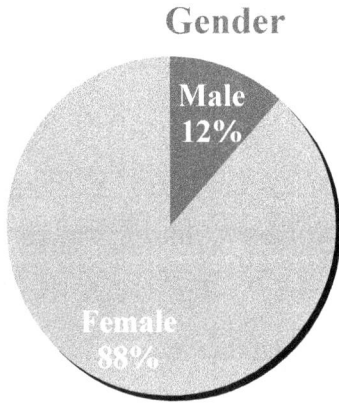

Fig. 3. Proportions of gender represented within the sample.

Age Groups

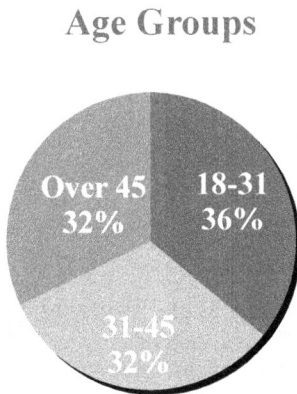

Fig. 4. Proportions of age represented within the sample.

Next, reliability of the subscales to be used in analysis was assessed using Cronbach's alpha test of reliability. Also known as the coefficient alpha, the Cronbach's alpha provides the mean correlation between each pair of items while accounting for the number of items in a scale (Brace, Kemp & Snelgar, 2006). Cronbach's alpha coefficients were evaluated using the guidelines suggested by George and Mallery (2010) where > .9 Excellent, > .8 Good, > .7 Acceptable, > .6 Questionable, > .5 Poor, and ≤ .5 Unacceptable. The Transformational leadership scale had the highest degree of reliability (α = .96), followed by the Engagement scale (α = .95); both indicated excellent levels of reliability. The Transactional leadership scale had a questionable degree of reliability (α = .61), and the Laissez Faire leadership scale had an acceptable degree of reliability. Table 2 presents Cronbach's alpha, means, and standard deviations for each subscale of interest, and Figures 5 and 6 provide means for each demographic group.

Table 2. Cronbach's Alpha Reliability for the Subscales of Interest

Scale	No. of items	α	M	SD
Transformational leadership	5	.96	3.80	0.93
Transactional leadership	8	.61	3.55	0.58
Laissez Faire leadership	4	.76	1.55	0.73
Engagement	17	.95	5.17	1.08

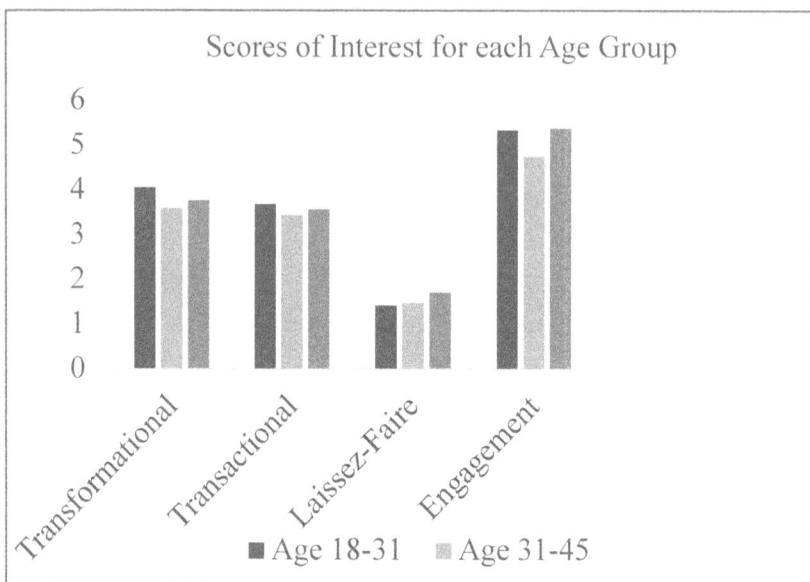

Scores of Interest for each Age Group

Age 18-31   Age 31-45

Fig, 5. Mean leadership scores for each age group.

Figure 5 depicts average leadership style and engagement scores for each age group. This figure provides a visual indication that, on average, participants scored Transformational and Transactional leadership styles with slight differences, and that these leadership scores were higher than average Laissez Faire scores. It also indicates that none of the leadership styles examined varied greatly between the age groups in question. On average, the age group of 18-31 and over 45 had similar Engagement scores, while the age group 31-45 had slightly lower Engagement scores. Engagement scores could be examined independent of leadership scores, as a different instrument was used to determine these averages.

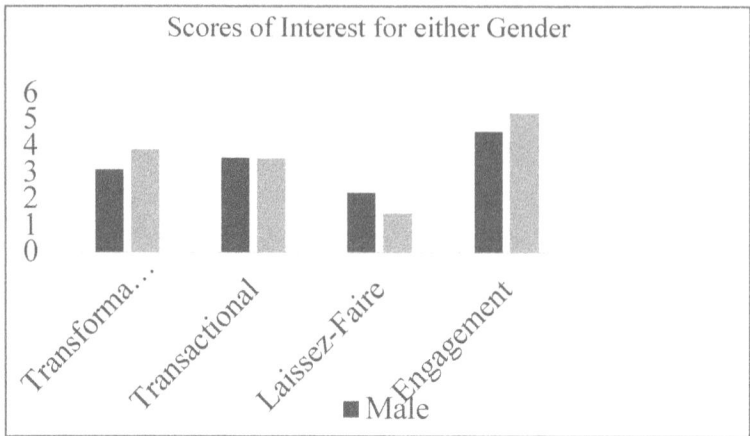

Scores of Interest for either Gender

6
5
4
3
2
1
0

Transformal... Transactional Laissez-Faire Engagement

■ Male

Fig. 6. Mean leadership scores for either gender.

Figure 6 depicts average leadership style and engagement scores for both genders. This figure provides a visual indication that, on average, female participants scored transformational leadership significantly higher than males. However, scores from both genders were average transactional leadership.

Both genders scored Laissez-faire leadership style lower than transformational and transactional leadership styles, but female participants scored Laissez-faire lower than their male counterparts did. Generally, females tended to have higher engagement scores than males.

Engagement scores could be examined independent of leadership scores, as a different instrument was used to determine these averages.

Analysis of the First Question

Analysis of the Questions

Does the level of employee engagement for clinical nurses correlate with transformational leadership styles?

To assess research question one, a Pearson product-moment correlation was conducted (Table 5) between employee engagement (as measured by the UWES) and transformational leadership style scores. Prior to analysis, the assumptions of linearity and homoscedasticity were assessed. The assumption of linearity was assessed using a scatterplot (Figure 7) between employee engagement scores and transformational leadership scores; this plot did not deviate strongly from a linear pattern, and the assumption was met. Homoscedasticity was assessed using a residuals scatterplot; the data did not deviate strongly from a random rectangular distribution, and this assumption was met as well.

Table 2. Pearson Product-Moment Correlation between Transformational Leadership and Engagement

Variable	Employee engagement
Transformational Leadership	.78***

Note. * indicates significance at the $p < .05$ level, ** indicates significance at the $p < .01$ level, and *** indicates significance at the $p < .001$ level.

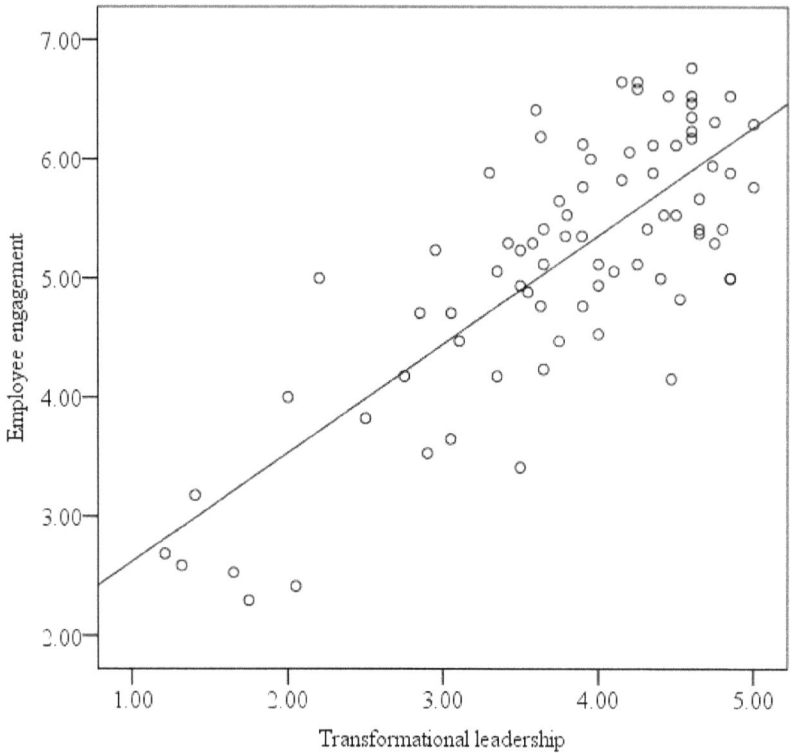

Fig. 7. Scatterplot of transformational leadership versus employee engagement.

Hypothesis One

H_01 stated that no correlation exists between employee engagement for clinical nurses and transformational leadership styles. Results of the Pearson product-moment correlation conducted between transformational leadership scores and employee engagement (Table 5) indicated a significant correlation (p < .001, $r(77)$ = .78). According to Cohen (1988), this corresponds with a large positive association. This positive association suggested that as transformational leadership scores increased, employee engagement increased as well. Results of this Pearson product-moment correlation are presented in Table 5, while a scatterplot of the two correlated variables are presented in Figure 7. The null hypothesis is rejected because the analysis indicated a statistically significant correlation between employee engagement for clinical nurses and transformational leadership styles.

Analysis of the Second Question

Does the level of employee engagement for clinical nurses correlate with transactional leadership style?

To assess research question two, a Pearson product-moment correlation was conducted (Table 6) between employee engagement (as measured by the UWES) and transactional leadership style scores. Prior to analysis, the assumptions of linearity and homoscedasticity were assessed. The assumption of linearity was assessed using a scatterplot (Figure 7);

between employee engagement scores and transactional leadership scores this plot did not deviate strongly from a linear pattern, and the assumption was met. Homoscedasticity was assessed using a residuals scatterplot; the data did not deviate strongly from a random rectangular distribution, and this assumption was met as well.

Table 3. Pearson Product-Moment Correlation between Transactional Leadership and Engagement

Variable	Employee engagement
Transactional Leadership	.47***

Note. * indicates significance at the $p < .05$ level, ** indicates significance at the $p < .01$ level, and *** indicates significance at the $p < .001$ level.

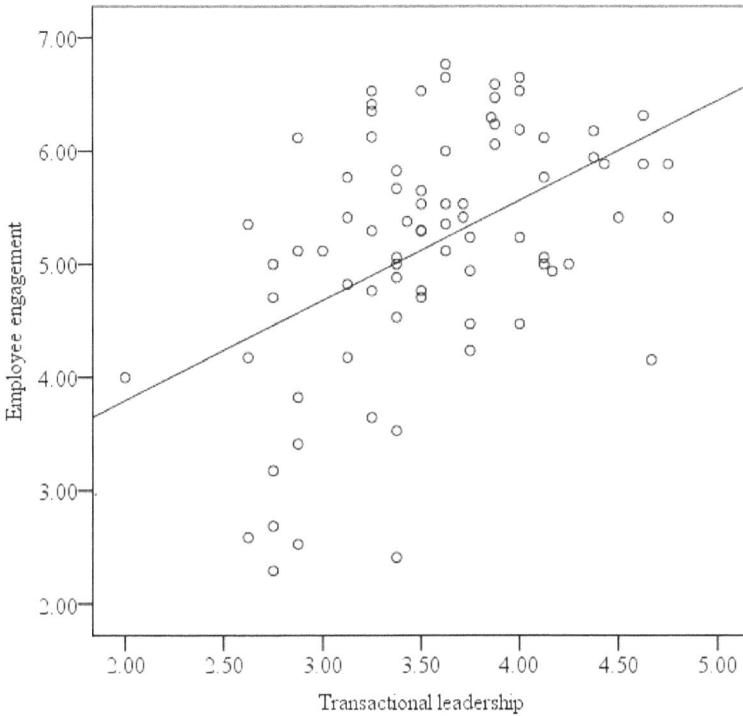

Fig. 7. Scatterplot of transactional leadership versus employee engagement.

Hypothesis Two

H₀2 stated that no correlation exists between clinical nurses' employee engagement and transactional leadership style. Results of the Pearson product-moment correlation between transactional leadership scores and employee engagement indicated a significant correlation

($p < .001$, $r(77) = .47$). According to Cohen (1988), this corresponds with a medium, but nearly large positive association. This positive association suggested that as transactional leadership scores increased, employee engagement increased as well. The results of this Pearson product-moment correlation are presented in Table 6, while a scatter plot of the two correlated variables are presented in Figure 7. The null hypothesis was rejected because the analysis indicated a statistically significant correlation between employee engagement for clinical nurses and transactional leadership style.

Analysis of the Third Question

Does the level of employee engagement for clinical nurses correlate with laissez-faire leadership style?

To assess research question three, a Pearson product-moment correlation was conducted (Table 7) between employee engagement (as measured by the UWES) and laissez-faire leadership style scores (as measured by the MLQ). Prior to analysis, the assumptions of linearity and homoscedasticity were assessed. The assumption of linearity was assessed using a scatterplot between employee engagement scores and

118

laissez-faire leadership scores (Figure 8). This plot did not deviate strongly from a linear pattern, and the assumption was met. Homoscedasticity was assessed using a residuals scatterplot; the data did not deviate strongly from a random rectangular distribution, and this assumption was met as well.

Table 4. Pearson Product-Moment Correlation between Laissez-Faire Leadership and Engagement

Variable	Employee engagement
Laissez-Faire Leadership	-.47***

Note. * indicates significance at the $p < .05$ level, ** indicates significance at the $p < .01$ level, and *** indicates significance at the $p < .001$ level.

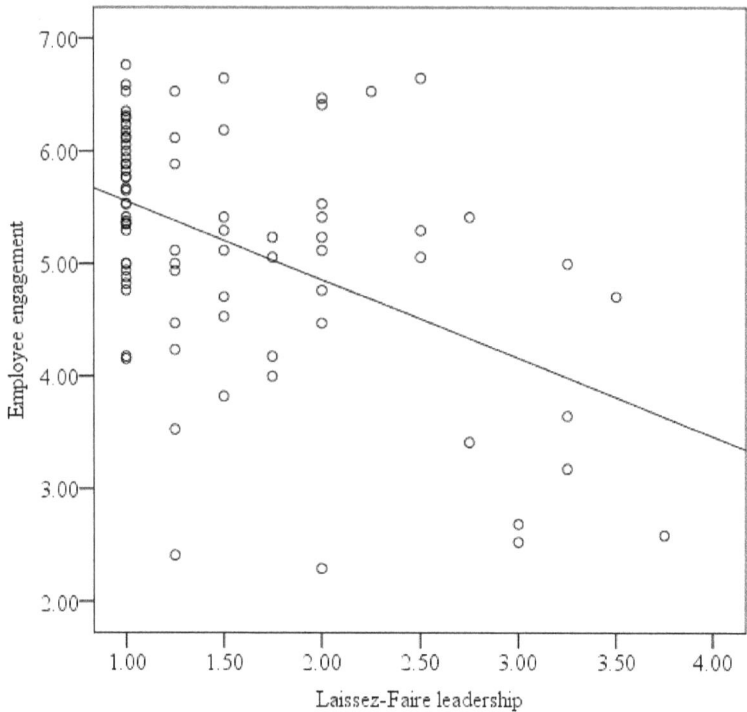

Fig. 8. Scatterplot of laissez-faire leadership versus employee engagement.

Hypothesis Three

H_03 stated that no correlation exists between clinical nurses' employee engagement and laissez-faire leadership style. Results of the Pearson product-moment correlation between laissez-faire leadership scores and employee engagement indicated a significant correlation $(p < .001, r(77) = -.47)$. According to Cohen (1988), this

120

corresponds with a medium, but nearly large negative association. This negative association suggested that as laissez-faire leadership scores increased, employee engagement decreased. Results of this Pearson product-moment correlation are presented in Table 7, while a scatter plot of the two correlated variables are presented in Figure 8. The null hypothesis was rejected because the analysis indicated a statistically significant negative correlation between employee engagement for clinical nurses and laissez-faire leadership style.

Leadership Practices and Engagement

All three leadership styles were analyzed together to determine the best leadership style to predict engagement. When all three are included in a model, they're able to control for one another's effects and explain how unique the predictors are. In this research, transformational leadership was uniquely able to predict engagement better than transactional and Laissez-faire leadership styles.

To determine how the three leadership (transformational, transactional and Laissez-faire) styles of interest together accurately predict the level of employee engagement for clinical nurses, a multiple linear regression was conducted between the three leadership styles and employee engagement. Prior to the analysis, the assumptions of the multiple linear regression were assessed. These assumptions include normality, homoscedasticity, and absence of multicollinearity. Normality was assessed by visual examination of a normal P-P plot; the plot did not deviate greatly from the normal line, and the assumption was met (see Figure 9). Homoscedasticity was assessed by visual examination of a residuals scatterplot; this plot did not deviate greatly from a rectangular (random) distribution, and this assumption was also met (see Figure 10); Tabachnick & Fidell, (2012). The absence of multicollinearity was assessed by examination of variance inflation factors (VIF); none of the predictor variables were greater than 10, and this indicated that the assumption was met (Stevens, 2009).

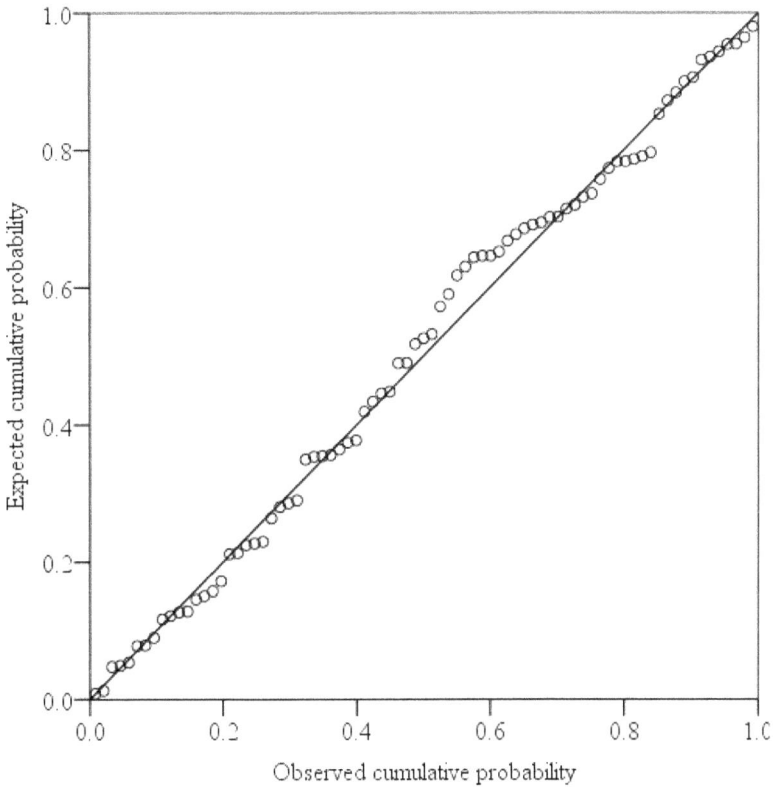

Fig. 9. Normal P-P Plot for transformational, transactional, and laissez-fair predicting.

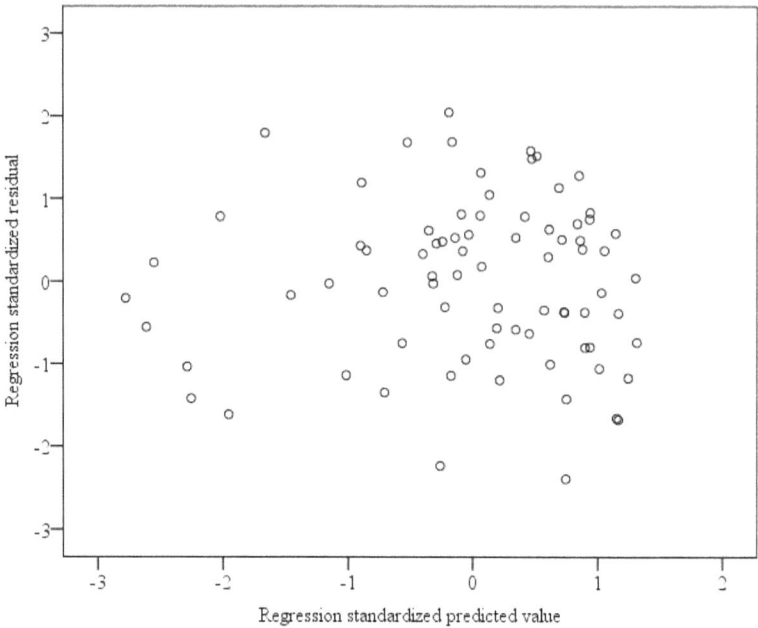

Fig, 10. Standardized residuals scatterplot for transformational, transactional, and laissez-faire predicting engagement.

Results of the multiple linear regression (table 8) indicated a significantly predictive model $F(3, 75) = 39.17$, $p < .001$, $R^2 = .61$). The R^2 value of .78 indicated a strong correlation between the predictor variables together with the outcome (Cohen, 1988). The R^2 value of .61 indicated that the three leadership styles together accounted for 61% of the variability in employee engagement. The resulting equation was: Level of employee engagement (Y) = 1.43 + 0.93(Transformational) + 0.03(Transactional) + 0.06(Laissez-Faire).

Next, individual predictors were assessed for predictive ability using t-tests. Only transformational leadership was a unique and significant predictor in the presence of transactional and laissez-faire leadership style scores ($t = 7.33$, $p < .001$). Examination of the B (unstandardized beta) value for Transformational leadership indicated that as transformational leadership scores increased by 1, employee engagement increased by 0.93 if all other predictors were held constant. No other leadership styles were significant predictors.

Results of the regression using the three leadership scores to predict engagement are presented in Table 8, and a partial plot for the one significant predictor is presented in Figure 11.

Table 5. Multiple Linear Regression with Transformational, Transactional, and Laissez-Faire Leadership predicting Employee Engagement

Source	B	SE	β	t	p	VIF
Transactional	0.03	0.17	.02	0.18	.854	1.53
Transformational	0.93	0.13	.80	7.33	.001	2.28
Laissez-Faire	0.06	0.14	.04	0.45	.655	1.68

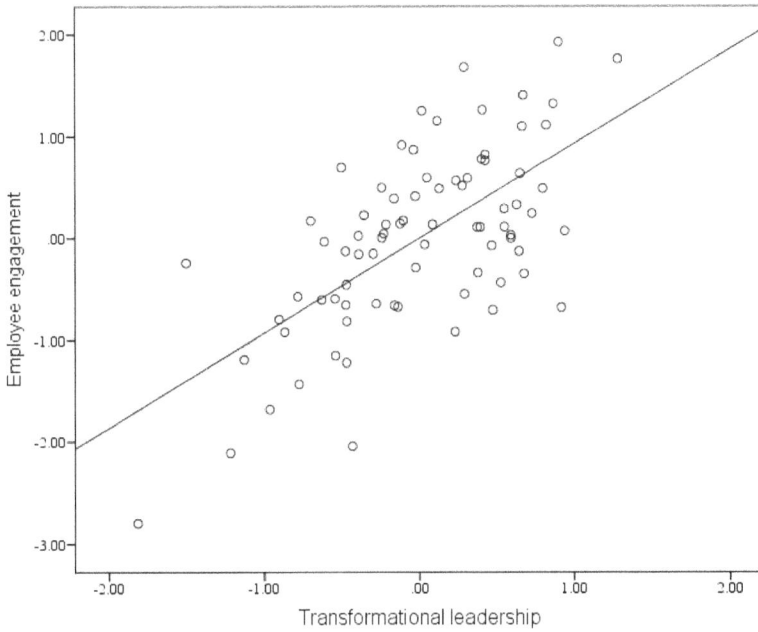

Fig. 11. Partial plot between transformational leadership and employee engagement holding transactional and laissez-faire leadership at a constant.

Summary

Chapter three explains the methodology selected for the research to examine potential relationships between the predictor and criterion variables of the study. Also included in Chapter three is sampling and the study sample size. An in-depth discuss of the data analysis is also explained to provide readers an explanation of how the study results and recommendations were reached. Descriptive statistics of collected data resulted in the data analysis that provided the empirical support for key findings, the conclusions, and recommendations following the study.

Additionally, data collected from clinical nurses was analyzed and the results presented in the chapter for an understanding of the entire picture painted in this book. The three research questions and their related hypotheses were derived from reviewed literature, and all the hypotheses examined were statistically significant. To assess each research question, correlation analysis was performed using a Pearson product-moment correlation conducted between employee engagement and the specific question's scores on leadership practice. Further, a multiple linear regression was conducted between the three leadership styles of interest and employee engagement.

Additionally, analysis of the data indicated that with regards to research question one, there is a strong linear relationship between transformational leadership style and employee engagement. Analysis for Research question two indicated a medium positive association that suggests that as transactional leadership scores increased, employee engagement increased as well suggesting a moderate statistically significant correlation between employee engagement for clinical nurses and transactional leadership. Analysis of the third research question indicated that there was a statistically significant correlation but largely negative relationship between Laissez-Faire leadership and employee engagements. The increase in Laissez-faire leadership style decreased employee engagement and vice-versa.

Multiple linear regression and F tests were conducted (Figure 10) to assess predictive levels of clinical nursing employee engagement in the presence of all three leadership styles. The results indicated that transformational, transactional and Laissez-Faire leadership styles together accounted for 61% of nursing employee engagement. Besides, t tests performed to determine the predictability of each individual leadership style in relation to clinical nurse engagement indicated that transactional and Laissez-Faire leadership styles were not relevant predictors of the level of nursing employee engagement (Table 8). When t value is above 2, it is said to be significant. Transformational leadership had a t value of 7.33, transactional 0.18 and Laissez-faire is 0.45 (Table 8).

Analysis of the study data further demonstrated that transformational leadership style alone can be used to predict the level of clinical nursing employee engagement because transformational leadership scores and employee engagement scores had a relationship of almost one-to-one. As transformational leadership scores increased by .001, nursing employee engagement scores increased by 0.93, an almost direct relationship (Table 8). Conversely, when transactional leadership scores increased by .854, nursing engagement increased by 0.03 and when Laissez-Faire scores increased by .655, nursing engagement scores increased by 0.06 (Table 8). When the other leadership styles are held constant, transformational leadership has a one-on-one relationship with nursing employee engagement. (Figure 11).

Analysis of the study data further revealed that clinical nurses between the ages of 18 and 31 scored transformational leadership highest in correlation with employee engagement (Figure 5).

Besides, transformational leadership scores in relation to employee engagement were higher for female respondents than their male counterparts (Figure 6). Implications of these findings will be discussed in Chapter 4.

IN-BETWEEN

Clear-Cut Facts

Findings from this quantitative correlation study revealed that when analyzed individually, each of the leadership styles correlate with clinical nursing employee engagement to a certain level. The study findings confirmed that transformational leadership scores and employee engagement indicated a significant correlation ($p < .001$, $r = .78$), and transactional leadership scores and employee engagement also indicated a significant correlation ($p < .001$, $r = .47$) which corresponded with a medium association only. Laissez-faire leadership scores and employee engagement also indicated a significant correlation ($p < .001$, $r = -.47$) that corresponded with a negative association which suggested the increase in laissez-faire leadership scores induced a decrease in employee engagement scores in Figure 8.

When the leadership styles (transformational, transactional and Laissez-Faire) were analyzed together to determine the best leadership style to predict engagement, findings of the study indicated that transformational leadership drowns both transactional and Laissez-faire leadership styles making them insignificant in predicting nursing employee engagement (Table 8). Transactional leadership style had a minimal correlation with clinical nursing employee engagement, and Laissez-faire leadership style negatively influenced clinical nursing employee engagement. Transformational leadership style had the highest level of predictability of clinical nursing employee engagement and had the highest correlation score with employee engagement.

Results of the research support earlier findings by some researchers that employee engagement correlates with transformational leadership styles. The conclusion of the study suggests that when all three leadership styles are included in a model; they are able to control for one another's effects and explain how distinctive the predictor of transformational leadership style was uniquely able to predict engagement better than transactional and Laissez-faire leadership patterns.

Results for Question One:

(1): Does the level of employee engagement for clinical nurses correlate with transformational leadership styles? The results of the first research question suggest the level of employee engagement for clinical nurses correlated significantly with transformational leadership style. This study and its results imply that uniquely, transformational leadership style could have a very positive impact on the level of engagement for clinical nurses in acute care settings. Consequently, it could contribute to slow or arrest the attrition of nurses from the profession, and curb the enduring nursing shortfall. This research identified a profile for transformational leadership that was highly associated with the level of engagement for clinical nurses.

Further, results of the study pointed to a tendency for the female nurses to demonstrate higher levels of employee engagement toward transformational leaders than their male counterparts. Male nurses equally experienced increased engagement when transformational leadership style was used. However, when analyzed alone, transactional leadership in relation to employee engagement was higher for male clinical nurses than for their female counterpart. Transformational leadership in relation to engagement was higher for clinical nurses aged 18 to 31 years (36%) and the over 45 years old (32% of participants).

The research findings of a significant correlation of transformational leadership style and clinical nurse engagement for the different age groups indicated that 68% (36% + 32%) of clinical nurse employees experienced high levels of work engagement when working with a transformational leader. This finding implies that the role of clinical leadership can critically influence the work environment and clinical nurses' engagement. Leaders affect the behaviors, attitudes and activities of personnel at various levels (Piersol, 2007). Healthcare organizations that desire to retain their valuable nursing human capital, reduce turnover, attrition and potentially the nursing shortfall in the current dynamic healthcare environment, should employ, train and encourage their leaders to adopt transformational leadership principles and practices.

An understanding of transformational leadership precepts and its relationship with the level of engagement for clinical nurses will allow healthcare organizations to experience enhanced staff loyalty, high productivity, and excitement about the work (Kerfoot, 2008). Leadership characteristics of hospital leaders and managers have often been acknowledged to fundamentally contribute to the efficiency of hospital units.

Since the leadership role assumed by clinical leaders is a contributory factor to staff attitudes, in order to reduce the rate of nursing attrition as an effort to combat the nursing shortfall in hospitals, health care organizations should address the leadership requirements of clinical leaders, and consider the introduction of transformational leadership training to middle and senior managers. Often, clinical leaders more naturally manifest transactional behaviors toward followers. Effective transformational leadership training will assist in preparing the next generation of clinical leaders with the necessary tools to manage successfully in the contemporary healthcare settings. Nurse Managers' implementation of the leadership role can significantly impact the work environment and organizational engagement.

Organizations with engaged, quality-driven, performance-centered, and satisfied employees obtain superior financial results and are better positioned to retain qualified and knowledgeable employees than organizations that have disengaged and dissatisfied workers (Little & Little, 2006).

Results for Question Two:

(2): Does the level of employee engagement for clinical nurses correlate with transactional leadership style? The results of the second research question indicate that employee engagement for clinical nurses correlated to a lesser degree with transactional leadership style. The results of the study demonstrated that female participants had slightly higher transformational leader scores than their male counterparts. However, both genders had similar average transactional leader scores. Both genders had lower Laissez-faire scores than transformational and transactional scores, while females had lower Laissez-faire scores than males.

This study and its results imply that nurse managers who adopted transactional leadership styles could have a moderate but positive impact on the level of engagement for clinical nurses and therefore help reduce the level of turnover in the hospital to a moderate extent. The empirical results for the research also indicated that although the transformational leadership style could uniquely predict high levels of clinical nurse engagement, and its leadership components are greater predictors of clinical nurses' engagement than transactional or laissez-faire leadership components, transformational leadership style and aspects of transactional leadership style can work together to achieve clinical nurses' engagement. This result provides support for recent findings by Bass and Avolio (2003), which suggested that elements of transformational and transactional leadership styles may result in the most effective leadership outcomes.

The results also partially supported the assertion by other researchers that although transformational leaders create a higher correlation between performance and motivation than transactional leadership, the best leaders are both transformational and transactional in their leadership styles. Further, transformational and transactional leadership styles are credited with increasing retention of workers and advanced as instrumental in the nursing shortage. The study data and analysis supported a positive relationship though in varying degrees between transactional and transformational leadership styles and the level of clinical nursing employee engagement.

Results for Question Three:

Does the level of employee engagement for clinical nurses correlate with laissez-faire leadership style? The results of the third research question demonstrated that the level of employee engagement for clinical nurses related negatively with Laisser-faire leadership. This implies that in healthcare organizations, including acute care hospitals where Laisser-faire leadership is practiced, leaders may be in need of reinvention and may require some fundamental orientation toward transformational and transactional leadership competencies.

Conclusion

Leadership research has suggested a positive relationship between leadership and organizational performance. To date, a small amount of research has considered leadership in the hospital environment and no research has considered leadership in relation with hospital clinical nurses' level of engagement. In identifying an empirical relationship between the level of clinical nursing employee engagement and three different leadership styles, this research makes a fundamental contribution to the study of employee engagement and leadership patterns at every level in the acute care hospital segment of the healthcare industry. These findings reinforce earlier invitations for nurse leaders to reframe their leadership orientation to obtain clinical nurses' satisfaction and commitment in order to gain engagement and curb nursing turnover and attrition rates. Responses to the three research questions indicated that, on average, leadership scores for transformational and transactional leadership were markedly higher than average laissez-faire scores. It also suggested that none of the leadership styles examined varied greatly between the age groups in question. Scores for Laissez-faire leadership were very low for all the age groups. On average, the age group of 18-31 and over 45 had similar Engagement scores, while the age group 31-45 had slightly lower Engagement scores.

The research confirmed that leaders in large acute care hospitals practice elements of both transformational and transactional leadership behaviors. The results also implied that in a dynamic environment, healthcare organizations that do not have transformational leaders could be at a competitive disadvantage.

CHAPTER FOUR

Engage to Conquer the Nursing Shortage

The study of nurses' engagement and the ways in which engagement and transformational leadership precepts correlate can proffer insights and provide leadership style suggestions for leaders of any healthcare organization, human resource professionals, and researchers. The current research provides empirical evidence that both transformational (to a very high degree) and transactional leadership (to a moderate degree) are positively related with clinical nurses' engagement. Following the conclusions of the study derived from the data analysis, there is a high degree of confidence in the following recommendations for healthcare and human resource leaders in their attempts to curtail the nursing attrition, increase engagement and retention in the profession.

As discussed earlier, a leader is a person of power and influence who gets people to do the things that he or she wants accomplished. Making people follow and accomplish more than their job responsibilities requires knowledge and skills set. Hence besides the ability to lead, the style that a leader uses to influence followers is critical to leadership effectiveness and organizational success. There is an abundance of leadership styles in theory and practice. Often, leaders utilize more than one style in their roles depending on the situational factors. Whatever style (s) a hospital leader uses, it is fundamental to reflect on the following leadership attributes to gain nurses' trust, respect, confidence, admiration, increase job satisfaction and retention levels, enjoy staff engagement, which all contribute to conquer the nurse shortage in your hospital.

Clinical Leadership Essentials

The current research on leadership styles and employee engagement in the healthcare industry is generalizable, and hence the recommendations are applicable to hospitals of all types, and leaders at every level in healthcare organizations. Hospitals generally face significant challenges including but not limited to human resource shortages on clinical units due to the persistent nursing shortage. Given the significant clinical human capital challenges hospitals around the nation are confronting, the role of hospital leaders continues to progress from the traditional transactional-based leadership pattern to more transformational leadership practices.

Core Values – Shared Values

Core values are an individual's most important beliefs. Several hospitals and organizations in other industries have "Value Statements" in their Employee Handbook. Organizations often communicate their core values during orientation for new hires, as an introduction to what the organization's beliefs are. Leaders' core values may differ from their organization's values. However, shared values are essential for corporations and employees to work well as good fits for each other. Values discussed in hospitals often include patient safety, compassionate care, dignity, quality, excellence, honesty, integrity, collaboration, team spirit, trust, respect, etc. Additionally, leaders may have personal espoused values including but not limited to open and honest communication, relationship building, fairness, justice, accountability, to mention a few.

Core values are a fundamental makeup of every human. Leaders manifest their core values in their daily decisions, interactions, behaviors, and communication with their followers. When nurses' values are in harmony with clinical leaders' or their organization's values, it means they share the same values, hence they have shared values. Shared values are important for individuals to collaborate efficiently toward achieving collective goals and personal growth. In hospitals, unfortunately for too long, nurses experienced in-fighting among themselves in what is known historically as "nurses eat their young" which became part of the "culture" in some hospitals. The absence of leaders who speak up against peer humiliation and bullying that comprises "eating their young" make it easy for some nurses to believe that clinical leaders are devoid of appreciable core values.

Nurses understand when their core values do not align with their leaders' or an organization's. That is when a leader and staff are not a good fit for each other. Leaders' core values play a prime role in their leadership style and is a contributory factor to nurse engagement and/or disengagement.

Bullying, intimidation, condescending behaviors, unfair and preferential treatments, favoritism, gossip, discrimination, dishonesty, whining, inappropriate and

146

general unprofessional conduct are a few of the serious core value issues confronting some clinical departments in hospitals. When these do not reflect the organization's shared values or culture, its senior leaders should seriously condemn such attitudes and behaviors in their clinical leaders and prominently argue for professionalism, a safe work environment, and respect for their staff.

In their 2016 article "Core Values." Amanat, Lingelbach & Schoen stated that core values are a leader's decision-making and conflict-resolution blueprint, arguing that they impact leaders' professional and social decisions. Besides, they posited that leaders' core values are significant in establishing interpersonal and organizational trust. Clinical leaders need to understand their personal core values and reflect on their potential effects on nurse's turnover intent, attrition, disengagement, and on the hospitals they serve.

Nurse participants in my research indicated high levels of engagement with leader's who use methods of leadership that align with their values such as acting in ways that build staff's respect and consider the moral and ethical consequences of decisions. Conversely, when a leader's core values do not align with theirs, they are less likely to feel compelled to engage in the organizational mission, and likely to resign due to dissatisfaction.

To curb the nursing attrition and shortfalls, hospital leaders need to articulate their core values and beliefs, and also implement them accordingly to improve nurse retention. Some literature has indicated that when leaders and followers have common or shared values, the potential for them to work successfully together in an engaging manner is very high. Such leaders easily get staff to take pride in their jobs and to perform more than expected. The research results suggest that clinical leaders that are most satisfying to staff lead cohesive and effective teams, and meet staff's work-related needs, talk about, and practice their most important values and beliefs.

Articulating and implementing core values by hospital leaders would be a giant step forward in the quest for improving nurse engagement. When value systems are incompatible, and in conflict, disengagement and or attrition are the results. Clinical leaders are in a unique position with maximum opportunity to engage nurses through appreciable common core values to establish the trust, respect, and confidence required for nurses to serve at their best.

The question from the study in this regard, recommended for hospital leaders to consider answering for themselves and their organizations is: Do clinical leaders reflect on their core values as part drivers of their work-related actions and decisions that affect nurse engagement? If so, what efforts or accomplishments were made?

Shared Core Values: The Canopy of Motivation

There are several pillars of motivation for nurses enumerated in this book. Shared values however, form the canopy for nurses' motivation. When a leader or an organization's espoused values marry with their employees', several other things in the relationship take shape benefiting the organization and its employees.

In "Voices from the field" nurses articulated personal values that when shared by clinical and organizational leaders, their motivation for collaborating with the leader to accomplish the hospital's mission peaks because they identify with the leader. The nurses indicated that it is easier to trust and respect leaders whose espoused values include honesty, fairness, justice, respect, open communication, supportiveness, transparency, teamwork, etcetera. When nurses' values align with their leaders' or vice versa, identification with the leader, motivation, commitment and engagement follow because of the foundation of shared values.

The Canopy of Motivation

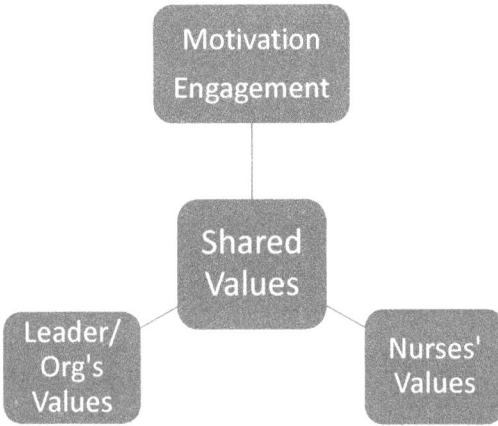

Fig. 12 Shared values- the canopy of motivation

Vision

Every hospital has a vision statement proudly written in their handbook, on their website, and in some rare cases, posted on a wall in the organization. Nurses indicated superior levels of engagement when their leader communicates a compelling vision of the future, discusses it optimistically and demonstrates enthusiasm about the work that needs to be accomplished for the organization to attain its vision.

Organizational theories have long discussed the influential role organizational vision plays on the individual and collective effectiveness of companies.

A construct without a clear-cut definition, vision has been painted by several authors to include descriptions or mental images shared among organizational members of what the organization should look like in the future. Leaders are responsible for explaining their organization's vision to employees. However, in some hospitals, years pass by without leaders communicating the organization's vision and other important information to followers. Twenty-first-century healthcare leaders must possess capabilities to think strategically, and carefully articulate a mission and a compelling vision in a manner that can generate trust, and inspire individual followers and teams to believe in the organization. Clinical leaders are responsible for communicating the hospital's vision with departmental employees.

It is important for hospital leaders to hold "Town Hall" style meetings either every six months or annually as preferred by the organization's leaders, to discuss the organization's vision with stakeholders, including clinical nurses. A clear articulation of a compelling organizational vision by leaders using such a forum is important to clinical nurses because it gives them an opportunity to understand the internal performance and functioning of their workplace, its financial stability or viability, its values and beliefs, expectations of how nurses should be treated by leaders, its external relationships with contractors, and its reputation as a healthcare provider in the community. "Town Hall" style forum gives nurses, especially night shift nurses, the chance to meet other hospital leaders, and have some of their questions answered. This is a forum that leaders can use to initiate true connections with clinical nurses.

Results of the research and an impressive body of empirical studies indicate that transformational leadership is an effective leadership style. Literature suggests that transformational leadership theory discusses vision-related leadership behavior and the effect on staff commitment and engagement. Results of this study indicate that communicating a compelling vision to clinical nurses can improve employee commitment and engagement. Clinical leaders do not have to be visionaries to be able to discuss the organization's vision with nurses. Notwithstanding, demonstrating a certain level of enthusiasm and confidence when discussing the vision is highly desirable.

Painting of the mental picture that represents the vision should be performed convincingly by a leader who can effectively communicate and demonstrate appropriate optimism about the organization's future.

Question: Do your hospital leaders create time during a year to communicate your hospital's vision to stakeholders including clinical nurses in a general open forum? How does that impact nursing engagement at your hospital?

Fairness and Justice

Without using a dictionary definition, fairness means to be impartial, avoiding favoritism and discrimination. Justice means to treat individuals fairly without taking sides. A leader's practice of fairness and justice is critical to gaining followers' trust and respect for the leader. The importance of trust in any relationship cannot be overemphasized, and in organizations, trust is the glue that binds leaders and followers in an incredible professional manner. Leaders who are trusted by their subordinates enable them to go above and beyond the required performance of their duties for the benefit of the organization. Current hospital workforce is highly diverse, multicultural and multigenerational. Clinical leaders' practice of fairness and justice among this very diverse group of nurses - of all ages and from all backgrounds is fundamental in establishing their credibility which engenders followers' trust. Trusting a leader's fairness and justice contributes to individual nurse's organizational membership satisfaction.

In hospital environments, it is easy for amateur, unskilled leaders to have favorites and to manifest their preference for certain members of their team. In "Voices from the nursing field" leadership fairness, unfairness, justice and injustice are recurrent themes. Mistrust of clinical leaders establishes quickly when nursing employees realize leaders have favorites among team members. The consequences of leader unfairness hurt multiple stakeholders and the organization. Conversely, *leadership fairness and just practices positively affect leader-employee relationship with crucial benefits on employees and organizational outcomes. Fairness and justice are morally correct leadership practices, and employee trust and respect often follow leaders who are impartial toward subordinates.*

Naturally, employees want to experience a great relationship with their leaders. However, enjoying an excellent relationship with leaders depends on a varied number of things from both sides. Nurses who indicated their leaders are fair and just, stated high levels of trust and respect for the leaders, and indicated both enjoy an excellent professional relationship as result. Besides, because of the established leader trust, nurses experience great outcomes such as high levels of job satisfaction, no absenteeism, commitment and engagement in their department's goals and the hospital's mission. The ultimate effect of leaders' fairness and justice is excellent organizational strategic outcomes from engaged workers.

Research suggests that transformational leadership style is related to job satisfaction, quality improvement, leader effectiveness and leader fairness that engenders trust in leadership. The research results indicate that transformational leadership style generates high levels of clinical nurse engagement. It is morally and ethically right for leaders to practice fairness. When leaders are clear about what employees can expect to receive when they attain performance goals and deliver equitably among staff when goals are accomplished, staff perceive the leader as being fair.

When leaders are consistent with fair work practices and do not consider certain team members as "special" to receive favors, employees' perception of the leaders as fair, just, honest, and trustworthy improves, thus engendering employee organizational citizenship behaviors such as engagement.

Trust in leaders plays a pivotal role in the theories of justice. Researchers usually discuss the four elements of justice namely, interpersonal justice, informational justice, distributive justice and procedural justice.

Although employees can differentiate between the different aspects of justice and their personal experiences with leadership justice, they usually discuss justice in the general sense of the word. Nurses have indicated that it is this general perception of justice that determines their level of trust for clinical leaders as just and fair brokers. An abundance of examples of situations exist in clinical settings that require leadership involvement, action or decision. Brokering each situation with justice and fairness is critical to employees.

Leaders that are perceived as fair and just, easily inspire employees to believe and trust them. In the general scheme of organizational strategy for staff retention, such leaders are capable of foiling employee turnover intentions and reduce the likelihood of staff shortfall. Leaders must be perceived as fair and just to gain nurses' trust, commitment, and engagement. Needless to emphasize that commitment, engagement and retention are needed to conquer the nursing attrition, turnover and shortage.

The Significance of Leadership Fairness and Justice.

Fig. 13 Leadership Fairness and Justice Outcomes

Individual Considerations

Individualized Consideration (IC) is one of the four characteristics of transformational leadership by Bass. It is a leaders' skill to support employees' individual needs (Yukl, 2010). IC is a leader's way of understanding each employee as an individual, different from all other team members. Nurse participants in the research responded favorably in high numbers to clinical leaders who consider and treat them as individuals rather than as members of a group. As humans, we each like to be considered and understood as individuals with idiosyncrasies even when we belong to a group or team.

Transformational leaders use individualized consideration to identify and support their employees as individuals with needs that are different from those of their peers. IC considers each member of a team as an individual and does not use the "one size fits all" theory in employee relations. As individuals on a team, each employee may have needs different from his or her colleagues. A nurse's individual needs could span from mentorship, education and training for performance improvement, to career development for advancement in the profession as a clinical leader.

Essentially, when clinical leaders understand nurses' individual needs and relate to them accordingly, it enhances their professional relationship and benefits each of them in varied ways. By tapping into the individual motivational vehicle of each nurse, healthcare leaders could easily forge recognition, rewards, training and development, or methods of communication that target the unique requirements of individual staff.

Hospital leaders may use individualized consideration to interact on a very high level with nurses, thereby engaging them and providing them job satisfaction. With the current cultural and generational diversity in the nursing workforce, clinical leaders who understand the importance of considering and treating each team member as different from the other, and adopt supportive practices to foster staff development and professional proficiency will be more effective in their leadership role. Such clinical leaders understand everyone on their team is different, functions differently with different paces, and have divergent professional needs for career advancement. Individualized consideration provides clinical leaders the opportunity to be better aligned to support, motivate and engage nurses as individual members of a clinical team.

Leaders are responsible for knowing and understanding what makes their employees tick, what motivates them, and tap into it to help generate excitement in their departments, work units and the organization in general. Healthcare leaders need to design engagement efforts that are unique to the idiosyncratic nature of individual employees.

Organizational effectiveness analyzes leadership through the relationship between leaders and employees because leadership is fundamental to ensuring an organization's effectiveness. Researchers posit that transformational leaders motivate team members through individualized consideration, development and maintenance of a positive and integral relationship. Clinical leaders who build individual relationships with each nurse through individual consideration have a higher potential to build strong connections with staff, trustworthy relationships, and encourage nurse engagement, and consequently obtain departmental and organizational effectiveness through engaged employees' high productivity.

Emotional Intelligence

Emotional Intelligence (EI) is an understanding of personal emotions, keeping the emotions in check effectively, and being aware of the emotional state of others. It entails awareness of self and others. In fast and stressful hospital settings, clinical leaders deal with an array of feelings that may interfere with modes and communication patterns. Clinical leaders require EI to be operationally effective in the daily business that involves interacting with several nursing personnel of diverse backgrounds and temperaments. Leaders' effectiveness in dealing with emotions when they run high determines their success in handling the daily challenges of leading a team, and establishing a culture of professional and respectful interactions.

Humans have a rational and an emotional mind that work collectively in decision-making situations. However, sometimes individual are more prone to use the emotional-decision-making mind before the rational reasoning reacts (Scott, 2013). In the "Voices from the

Nursing Field," nurses recount disheartening situations where clinical leaders yell frantically at them and even at department managers in the presence of witnesses such as visitors and families. Possessing a good dose of EI is significant for clinical leaders who not only interact with managers, supervisors, nursing staff and patients, they also interact with pleased and displeased families who convey their emotions during such interactions. A superior level of leaders' EI is essential to interact successfully with all healthcare stakeholders, and even more critical to effect a positive, caring, respectful and safe work environment that is empowering and engaging to nursing staff.

Emotional Intelligence requires self-discipline, empathy, listening skills and continuous efforts to think prior to acting or reacting to a situation, a comment, or a complaint. An emotionally intelligent clinical leader will be better-prepared and more efficient in assessing and dealing with work-related emotional issues in culturally and generationally diverse work environments within hospitals. Besides, with superior levels of EI, clinical leaders would lead teams more understandingly and empathetically. An understanding and empathetic clinical leader has a higher potential to connect with nurses, gain their respect, trust, and incite their engagement and active participation in the organization's mission.

Coach-Educate-Mentor-Train (CEMT)

Coaching, education, mentoring and training (CEMT) are empowering because of the potential to enhance nurses' knowledge and skills. Improved nursing skills through coaching and mentoring or training provides nurses the capabilities to plan, make decisions and solve patient care problems more swiftly, independently, and proficiently. Professional proficiency increases self-esteem. CEMT are a combination of highly motivational factors for nurses' engagement in an organization's mission.

My research participants indicated a preference for clinical leaders who spend time teaching, coaching and mentoring them. The study results indicate that nursing engagement is possible when leaders dedicate time to coach and teach them acceptable professional standards of nursing practice. Coaching is a professional development strategy used for multiple reasons including competency and performance improvement, empowerment and professional enhancement.

Clinical leaders are often tasked to the brim with multiple responsibilities. As a result, clinical leaders in big acute care or university teaching hospitals with large nursing units of 30 to 45 beds each, often dispose of very limited or no time to appropriately coach and mentor new, struggling or inexperienced nurses. Human resource professionals on the organizational development team of such big hospital systems usually coach, educate, mentor and train employees. Exceptional leaders often create time to play the role of coach and/or mentor in big hospital systems. Notwithstanding, in smaller hospitals, it is not impossible for the clinical leader to assume the role of coach and mentor for nursing performance improvement. Worth noting is the fact that results from my research suggest that coaching nurses would result in nurses' engagement.

Nursing education entails learning nursing sciences in theory on academic campuses, and learning practical nursing during hospital rotations in clinical settings. This has not proven to be sufficient to prepare nurses to "hit the ground running" upon graduating

167

nursing school. After providing general hospital orientation and unit-specific orientation to newly hired inexperienced nurses, clinical leaders need to assess their strengths and weaknesses to determine if some, or all of them need more practical education for competent practice. A profession that deals with consumers' lives, some nursing errors are potentially fatal. It is responsible for hospital leaders to ascertain that nurses are very competent to independently assume patient care responsibilities prior to assigning them care duties. Clinical nurses want to successfully provide safe care, in addition to appropriately prioritize care, assess clinical issues from multiple viewpoints, and develop their professional strengths. This may partially explain why my study respondents indicated high levels of energy at work for leaders who spend time coaching them.

Coaching post unit-specific orientation is not necessarily for new nurses only. Newly hired nurses could be experienced nurses moving from one specialty to another. For example, nurses transferring from acute rehabilitation units to an acute surgical or critical care unit, or a nurse transferring from an acute medical unit to a cardiac catheterization or oncology unit may also need and benefit from several weeks of coaching with designated preceptors. Depending on the organization's size and coaching need, a clinical director or clinical leader may coach nurses. Examples of such instances include coaching for improved job performance, on how to handle challenging situations on the unit with patients and colleagues, and/or about policies and procedures, and acceptable standards of clinical nurse practice, etcetera.

Successful Coaching Plan

Whatever the case maybe, clinical leaders should identify the specific needs to coach nurses in the departments they lead. Coaching nurses for performance improvement and competency requires strategy for the coaching to be beneficial and successful. The rationale for coaching or the need must be clearly stated. For example, coaching may be needed to attain strategic goals for clinical employees including newly hired nurses. For coaching to be successful, it should be purpose-driven, with coaching goals and objectives, coaching schedule with beginning and end points, post coaching assessment period, and a post-coaching performance evaluation plan and feedback.

Coaching should be performed by a trusted, compassionate, non-judgmental, nurturing and supportive individual who would assist staff in achieving set goals; with a vision and a flair for nurse advocacy. He or she should be a preceptor with clinical expertise to facilitate the nurses' development as confident, self-directed, empowered, safe clinical care providers.

Training Cost Considerations

In the strategic plan of certain healthcare organizations, improving the clinical knowledge and skill level of inexperienced nursing staff is an evident item. Notwithstanding, it is not a secret that due to costs for training, some healthcare organizations and leaders argue against continuous coaching and training of newly hired nurses after six to eight weeks of unit-specific orientation with a preceptor. However, the cost of errors and the cost for patients' lives surpass the cost for providing more training for nurses who need it to improve performance and competency levels to provide safe care. After the six to eight weeks of department-specific orientation, it is not uncommon to realize that some nurses still "don't know what they don't know" in clinical practice.

Training and coaching bedside nurses is very empowering. It advances their potential to be successful in nursing practice with improved knowledge and skills set. With enhanced knowledge, the coached nurses' effectiveness and strengths as clinical experts also improve. Improved nursing skills through coaching and training provides nurses the capabilities to plan, make decisions and solve patient care problems more swiftly, independently, and proficiently. Professional proficiency increases self-esteem.

These are a combination of highly motivational factors for nurses' engagement in an organization. Coaching nurses is, therefore, a win-win for the coached nurses and the organization. Advantages to the organization's human and financial resources from the coaching are invaluable.

The Case for Transformational Leadership

Transformational leaders are said to help employees develop their strengths and therefore empower them. Nurses affirmed in the study that they prefer clinical leaders who coach, educate and mentor them for performance and competency improvement. Coaching employees is empowering. It improves their knowledge and gives them the tools for success in their profession.

Two of the four components of transformational leadership per Bass, "Intellectual Stimulation" and "Individualized Considerations" are elements of the leadership style that speaks to developing employees. The transformational leader identifies the unique needs of individual employees to coach and mentor them accordingly. Transformational leaders use questions and scenarios to incite critical thinking skills and stimulate the intellect of their subordinates. In the changing healthcare landscape, effective clinical leadership skills are critical for ensuring nursing retention and engagement needed to enhance quality of care and patient satisfaction. Bass asserted that transformational leaders are better positioned to attain higher staff performance by stimulating and transforming followers' beliefs and aspirations. This study results confirm some of Bass's assertion about transformational leadership by demonstrating that transformational leadership style is better suited to achieve high levels of clinical nurses' engagement than the other leadership styles in the study.

Bass wrote that transformational leadership results in higher levels of employee performance than that produced by transactional leadership. Leadership authors have cited transformational leadership style as consistently associated with employee motivation and positive employee-leader relationships, employee effectiveness and client satisfaction in comparison with non-transformational leadership styles. Transformational leaders are effective leaders. Hence, they are appropriate, desirable and suitable for nursing environments because they advocate empowerment of nurses and foster staff motivation.

Pillars of Motivation for Engagement

Motivation is a concept that could be intrinsic or extrinsic. Intrinsic motivation is personal and internal. It comes from within. Extrinsic motivation is from external stimuli. Nurses are not short of intrinsic or internal motivation to do their jobs. However, with the enduring challenges of nursing attrition and shortages confronting hospitals in the nation, the intrinsic motivation of clinical nurses needs to be supported with extrinsic motivators to gain their commitment and engagement.

Despite its self-satisfying potential, clinical nursing is tedious, and nurses deserve acknowledgment for the job they do, and motivation to continue performing at their best. Clinical Nursing is a stressful profession that involves the potential for making different kinds of mistakes. This makes it easy for some leaders to focus their attention on the errors, irregularities, outlier issues, deviations from standards of practice, failures needing improvement, complaints, and what is wrong. While performance improvement discussions and activities are highly critical in hospitals for varied reasons, leaders need to also celebrate what is good, very good, and what is great in/about their nurses daily. A daily celebration of nurses would make them feel valued, recognized and motivated to perform better and give in their best to fulfill the hospital's mission and vision.

Clinical leaders are responsible for all their departments' quality of care and cost containment efforts. Working short-handed is detrimental to the provision of safe and high quality nursing care, treatment and services. Errors that could result from working short are very costly, and turnover is also very costly. Clinical leaders require the skills and ability to motivate nurses to achieve

174

job satisfaction and to perform the duties excellently to obtain optimal quality of patient care, patient satisfaction as well as contain costs. Motivated and engaged workers are highly productive which makes it quite essential to have motivated nurses whose productivity level is fundamental to the bottom line of hospitals.

Motivated nurses are energetic, focused, dedicated and are less liable to be absent or make errors that cost hospitals millions of dollars annually. Motivation is a cost containment strategy that hospital leaders need to explore, instead of reducing essential staff such as nurse unit secretaries and care aids and technicians. Motivating nurses is critical to retention, commitment, and engagement. The reverse has multiple disadvantages including turnover, bedside nursing shortages and all the negative effects of the shortage. Leaders do not need to move mountains to motivate nurses. Very simple, non-transactional, and sometimes humanistic measures may suffice to motivate nurses. Besides, nurse motivation is needed to engage staff for enhanced delivery of safe, high-quality patient care.

Role Model Motivation

Leaders are often the role model for their staff. Leading by example is important, and often, staff adopt the attitudes and behaviors of their leaders. To motivate nurses, clinical leaders need to look, feel and act motivated. Clinical leaders who demonstrate enthusiasm, a positive attitude, can work side-by-side staff pleasantly, smile, greet staff warmly, accept responsibilities without whining, set the tone for employees.

A motivated leader is a positive influence on employee's motivation. In clinical settings, attitudes can become easily infectious and could spread fast. Leaders who consistently create a positive work atmosphere, demonstrate motivation and dynamism, inspire and motivate their staff. Conversely, clinical leaders who put up "an attitude" toward staff, are boisterous, bully and talk down to their staff, complain often, are generally unpleasant and grumpy, are killers of employee motivation. Leaders should not expect staff to be enthused and motivated in a work environment that is not conducive to function in. Some nursing units have been said to be "unable to keep their staff."

When turnover is high, directors of human resources or the senior leaders over the high turnover departments need to begin asking pertinent questions about the leadership style employed by the clinical leader. Further, motivational strategies of the leader if at all existent, should also be assessed. The recommendation here cannot stress enough how important it is for clinical leaders to motivate nurses by leading by example and exhibit motivation.

Sincere "Thank You" – A Pat.

Leaders do not need to wait for a big moment to congratulate their staff for a job well done, or for meeting performance expectations. Employ the "See it, Say it" practice with nurses on the job in a "Just in Time" manner. When a leader witnesses a nurse's good work, or are informed of something commendable a team member did, he or she should create time to acknowledge and recognize the staff irrespective of the nature of the good deed. No good deed is too small to reward with a nice pat on the back and a simple, and sincere "Thank You." This is positive reinforcement which makes employees feel and take more pride in their work.

A leader's personal acknowledgment for employee's good work is inspirational, a moral boost and it is motivating. It validates the employee's efforts as having purpose and being meaningful. This indicates to the employees that the leader values and appreciates their individual contributions as team members. This is simple to do, and it is motivating. Transformational leaders use skilled communication to nurture their employees, build their self-esteem, empower and engage them (Bass). Schaufeli and Bakker contend that when employees find the work they do meaningful and of purpose, they are dedicated. Leaders should make it a habit to immediately praise employees that do the smallest good work, as well as staff that goes above and beyond in a big way. A sincere praise and "thank you" are staff motivators. They are like huge gifts wrapped in beautiful small packets that cost nothing more than sincere words of appreciation.

Make Work Engagements Fun

It is natural to appreciate fun environments and fun times. This explains why some clinical leaders have quarterly "Friday Fiesta" or "Happy Hour with staff" to discuss work-related matters. Some very skilled clinical leaders reserve a "no fee private room" to host staff meetings while having fun out of the work environment. In "Nursing Voices from the Field" several nurses explained how fun and relaxing it is to discuss items on an agenda with a hospital leader, away from the hospital grounds. The nurses indicated their appreciation for the clinical leaders who put effort to hold meetings in a fun atmosphere.

Several nurses confirmed that this is motivational, asserting they often look forward to their department head's off campus quarterly meetings.

Clinical leaders should think of holding staff meetings outside the hospital grounds where staff can participate while having fun. This type of casual-social but professional gathering lets employees understand you want them to relax and enjoy with peers while discussing work. Nurses who experience this fun quarterly say they look forward to it and remember it as "the team's meeting time with a nice pinch of team fun, away from stressful walls." This is said to be a stimulator of staff motivation.

Quality of Work-Life Balance

Demonstrating sincere interest in the quality of nurses' work life is fundamental and motivating because it demonstrates to them their leader's advocacy for them as invaluable assets to the hospital, who are appreciated and treated with understanding and respect. Think about it simply for a moment, without nurses, hospital units will not function and patients will not receive care. It follows therefore that nurses who take care of other individuals deserve quality in their work life. Leaders' promotion of quality of work life for nurses is a powerful motivator in the profession.

Understandably, hospitals are highly busy places and nursing units symbolize that business. It is sometimes very challenging to find time to speak thoughtfully with a nurse. However, this does not have to be lengthy or take up much time. It is very important for leaders to interact with their staff interpersonally and more personally to demonstrate their sincere interest in their life, health and well-being as individuals, and in their family's well-being.

A leader's warm and caring interactions with nurses is motivational because it lets them understand that the leader is empathetic, that nurses are appreciated as social beings and are cared for as the rock and strength of the hospital. Sincere, warm interactions between a leader and a nurse can go a long way. Naturally, employees trust and respect leaders who show sincere interest in their well-being. Trust in a leader leads to improved job satisfaction, decreased absenteeism, reduced turnover intent, and ultimately curbs attrition. Trust and respect for a leader engenders engagement and positive job outcomes for nurses. Additional advantages for this simple gesture of staff motivation are innumerable and intersect to include increased quality of care and patient outcomes, and human and financial resources for the organization.

Offer Various Incentives

Also of importance are staff incentives that include some cost. Depending on the healthcare organization, financial costs for staff incentives is part of a department's budget. Motivators of this nature include gift cards of minimal amounts per the hospital's gift policy, meal cards, movie tickets, ice cream gift card, chocolate, cake or dessert specialized store cards which are often very popular with nurses who have young children, nieces, nephews or grandchildren. Clinical leaders could incentivize nurses who go an extra mile for the good of the team and the organization by gifting him or her one of such a token of appreciation.

It is beneficial for clinical leaders to know individual staff members well enough, and to understand what would token of acknowledgment would be more meaningful or relevant to him or her. Nurses with young children may prefer an ice cream or cupcake store gift card, while a bachelor, bachelorette or spinster may prefer movie tickets for one or two. Some nurses have received massage gift cards worth $50.00, while others have earned a dinner date for two with the clinical leader, and yet others have earned a gift card to their favorite scrubs store. Knowing individual nurses well could help make this type of incentive successful. Some clinical leaders give out "Thank You" cards with sweet, brief handwritten notes to acknowledge their nurses.

Employing "other incentives" motivation techniques should be consistent, fair, long-lasting and done appropriately and professionally. Understanding each nurse's comfort level with overt or covert motivating techniques is also critical to make it meaningful. The leader should know the staff well individually prior to dispensing any type of motivator. Not everyone likes a fanfare about them so openly congratulating or acknowledging such individuals would be counter-productive. It is critical to tailor extrinsic motivators according to individual preferences, and certainly, do not use incentives or motivators of any kind to instill competition among nursing staff. The profession is already very stressful, and nurses do not need to compete against each other for professional recognition by their managers. Rather, they need to work with each other in a supportive fashion toward a collective goal and the objective of incentives and motivators should reflect such.

Authentic Self-Scheduling

Many years ago, some hospital leaders decided nurses could write their shift preferences on their manager's draft schedule, and that would suffice to guarantee each nurse would work the selected day/shift. According to "Voices from the Field", in some hospitals, this was not well rolled out, and several nurses did not quite understand the full implications of providing the department manager their preferred work days on the draft schedule. Chaos followed in some clinical nursing departments when schedules for three consecutive months were printed and several nurses' realized their suggested, selected and preferred work days had not been honored.

A great incentive or motivator to keep nurses in the profession, the "Self-scheduling" program failed initially in several hospitals and nursing units before clinical leaders returned to the drawing board to perfect the program and educate nurse managers on "effective program roll out." Self-scheduling, as it is known, is a powerful motivator in nursing, all things being equal. However, it is important for it to be a true self-scheduling for nurses to feel its true positive effect. Leaders should explain the full implications of the nursing self-schedule to preclude potential issues arising from misunderstanding of the program. A significant motivator, some "Voices from the nursing field" indicated:

"I love nursing because at our hospital, I get to work when I chose to work and be off with my family when I chose to. I usually work my three twelve hour shifts together so I can be off the rest of the time. That means I could be off for five or even seven consecutive days if I want to. The flexibility of self-scheduling is priceless when it is true self-scheduling."

Others stated the following, summarily:

"There is nothing like working for three straight days at a hospital and work another three straight days at another hospital. You easily keep two jobs without worrying that you will let one hospital down. This is the beauty of nursing self-scheduling. Our manager honors our requests. We all follow a pattern and it is first come, first served. We complete the schedule according to the number of nurses already signed up for a certain day, how many nurses are scheduled daily during the week and on the weekends. It was very well explained to us at both hospitals, and it is working greatly for me and my family."

Utilizing true self-scheduling to motivate nurses is a possibility for clinical leaders. All around the nation, nurses see the self-scheduling process as a serious bargaining power for hospitals to utilize in hiring talented nurses. Hospital leaders who have not appropriately implemented true nurse self-scheduling in clinical departments have an opportunity to do it correctly and experience its motivating effects on nurses.

Empowerment

Empowerment is a term used situationally and in a variety of circumstance. In hospitals, empowering nurses entails practices such as providing training for performance improvement and success, mentoring for independence, providing the information, material and equipment needed to work more efficiently, and effectively communicating pertinent information. Nurse empowerment is a motivator in the profession.

Further, nurses have indicated that participation in decision-making processes, involvement in hospital committees, unit-based councils, change management processes, managing and collaborating with colleagues on departmental projects to share their skills and knowledge, sharing their perspectives and viewpoints on potential departmental or organizational changes, and receiving incremental responsibilities are highly empowering and motivating. It behooves hospital leaders to empower individual nurses accordingly to motivate and engage them in their organization's mission.

Teamwork

It is important for leaders to make the work environment inviting by employing meaningful and satisfactory motivation techniques that can help stop the nurse attrition and the consequent shortage. Work environments should be safe and friendly places. In hospitals especially, nurses spend very long hours at work, and it is frustrating to practice in an unsafe and unprofessional "non-friendly" environment according nursing voices. A clinical nurse leader several years ago, I told my team:

"Our department is home away from home. We all spend so many hours here at work, so we should work collegially and as a team toward our collective goal. As humans, we all want and like happiness. We all want to be happy here at work. Let's make it happen for ourselves and each team member."

Clinical leaders can create a friendly work environment for nurses using many techniques including, but not limited to promoting teamwork, encouraging team cohesiveness, upholding a culture of respect, open communication, and professionalism. While in clinical leadership, several nurses consistently indicated teamwork and team cohesiveness to be paramount motivators to them. The following comes from the collection of "Voices from the Nursing Field":

"For me to get up early in the morning to go spend 12 hours on my feet caring for patients at a hospital, there better be very good teamwork on the unit. Teamwork is what motivates me more than anything, to do this job. We have a solid team, never short of help for each other. We come together every day to provide quality service for our patients. The teamwork alone is enough motivation for me and several of my colleagues. Knowing that we are a strong cohesive team, mutually supportive peers and that we are all in this together, keeps our morale high."

Another nurse and very dear friend's voice from the field was as follows:

"I work on a forty-five-bed unit. Nurses do not work for a long time there. It is not a unit where any reasonable nurse would stay for long, but whenever you try to transfer to another department, she (the department leader) would not sign the paperwork required for the transfer. Her leadership skills leave much-to-be-desired. The charge nurse sits up front, is condescending and rude, and never helps, or to be fair, only helps in emergencies.

Each nurse is for him or herself, there is no teamwork, and the assignment is never fair. It is a very rough unit. I have requested a transfer to a different department but there is no hope that will happen soon. Right now, I am thinking of alternatives. No doubt the unit is always so short staff and no one lasts for long here."

Teamwork is essential in nursing as a motivator. Clinical departments with silos are dysfunctional and a recipe for disaster at the hospital. Establishing clinical departments on the foundation of team spirit and collective effort is a selling point to nurses because of the multiple benefits of team-oriented workplaces. Working as a team in nursing is unifying, it creates understanding among colleagues, establishes a collegial work environment, and makes the work less stressful. Positive nursing team spirit means the nurses all have each other's back in a collaborating relationship for employee and patient safety and satisfaction.

Nurses are highly motivated and engaged in departments where everyone comes together as a team to assist colleagues complete the day's work, answer call lights, take telephone orders and transcribe them on behalf of a team member, page a doctor on behalf of a peer, go to the lab and pick up blood for transfusion on behalf of a colleague, and administer treatment to a patient on behalf of another team member etcetera. Teamwork is powerful. It motivates nurses, increases team cohesiveness, positive team dynamics, job satisfaction, and encourages engagement. Teamwork is a win-win for clinical leaders and nurses because it reduces staff dissatisfaction and attrition, it decreases several patient-care risks, and improves the safety and quality of patient care.

Culture of Respect

When an organization's culture and its employees' personal values marry, the relationship could be very fulfilling, motivating and long lasting. The reverse would cause the complete antithesis to follow. Within large organizations, sometimes cultures develop in small pockets and could sustain due to dynamics created by the informal organization. As a result, in some acute care hospitals, it is not uncommon to experience divergent and opposing organizational cultures within the different hospital departments.

To stop the nurse bleed by attrition, encourage commitment and engagement in the nursing workforce, clinical leaders should establish and sustain a culture of

190

respect for and among nurses. Retention of skilled, committed and engaged nurses in healthcare requires strong, decisive clinical leaders with intolerance for acutely disrespectful nurses whose inappropriate behaviors negatively influence their peers, the profession and patients.

Workforce violence is not a new word to nurses. Some nursing departments are breweries for workplace bullying language and behavior, and hostility among nurses. Unwelcoming, oppressive behaviors of some veteran nurses toward newer, unseasoned nurses are experiences voiced by uncountable nurses in the collection of *Voices from the nursing field*. In some nursing units where the culture permits, some nurses speak condescendingly to newly hired and inexperienced peers, and demonstrate inappropriate behaviors with impunity. Clinical leaders are responsible for preventing and stopping noxious attitudes, languages and behaviors among nursing colleagues, especially in the departments under their leadership. As nursing superiors, clinical leaders need to set a cultural tone of respect among nursing professionals and all stakeholders.

Hospital leaders are responsible for standardizing an organizational culture of respect among all stakeholders. Besides, clinical leaders at the head of the profession require attentiveness to verbal abuse among employees, and actively utilize their power and skills to institute a culture of respect among nurses.

Nursing workplace hostility is neither a recipe for commitment nor engagement. The sarcastic language, passive aggressive, to general unprofessional behaviors that are devoid of peer-empowerment among nurses are contributory factors to nurse absenteeism and ultimate attrition. Besides, nursing workplace violence has multiple negative effects on the abused nurses, team dynamics, on patient safety, quality of patient care, and on the organization.

Further, it contributes to nursing job dissatisfaction, attrition and ultimately, the shortage. A culture of respect implanted by powerful clinical leaders is imperative for resolving this enduring issue. To build a culture of respect among nurses as a motivator, leaders should demonstrate zero tolerance of peer bullying and/or mutual disrespect, lead by example, and institute or appropriately implement policies that underscore intolerance for a hostile work environment.

Hospital leaders are responsible for setting and enforcing expectations for employee behaviors. They set the tone for a culture of respect by practicing respectful communication themselves, exemplifying inclusiveness, and upholding professionalism and collegial support. Working in a culturally respectful and inclusive work environment is a nurse motivator, critical to nursing job satisfaction and potential work engagement.

Communication Skills

Hospitals need committed and engaged nurses to provide premium quality care to their clients. The continuous nursing attrition and nursing shortage make it challenging for hospitals to accomplish their strategic quality and patient safety goals. The communication styles of clinical leaders play a fundamental role in nurses' motivation, job satisfaction and engagement because nurses consistently discuss their need for leaders who possess effective communication skills.

Effective communication is a process of exchanging information, knowledge, ideas and thoughts in a way that is respectful and acceptable by the parties involved in the communication. To effectively communicate, an individual has to deliver a message with clarity, and also listen to the interlocutor(s) so that all parties feel heard and understood. Effective communication entails delivering information to the right person, in the right manner, at the right time, and by the right person.

Healthcare leaders need to place emphasize on effective communication within their teams by using communication strategies founded on clarity, respect, openness, transparency, and consistency.

Nurses' engagement would be best nurtured when leaders' communication styles are reflective of an organizational culture of respect. Positive workplace leader-follower relationship depends on acceptable leader communication skills, effective communication, among other things. Researchers posit that great leaders utilize communication as a solid impetus for building and sustaining trust in employees, and trusted leaders are more likely than not, to gain the admiration, commitment and engagement of employees.

It has become even more important for clinical leaders to understand the significance and implications of effective communication skills because current nursing environments are multigenerational and multicultural, with an increasing presence of diversity in all its forms. Each of the diverse groups of nurses may have a preferred method of communication, which could be very challenging for leaders who communicate better using the old-fashioned face-to-face communication but are less effective when using e-mail, text, instant messenger, Teams, or telephone.

Professional development for clinical leaders requiring lessons in appropriate and effective communication skills is recommended for hospitals with untrained, young, new and/or inexperienced clinical leaders. Development of clinical leaders' communication skills cannot be over-emphasized, considering the current diversity in the nursing workforce, and the potential for misinterpretation of a leader's communication method and/or style by one or many of the diverse groups in the department. The benefits of effective communication in the current multicultural, multigenerational and highly diverse nursing workforce are multifold —(1) possessing and demonstrating effective communication skills gives nurse leaders the potential to deliver information to their team members respectfully, and with clarity; (2) effectively communicating with the teams is a morale booster for team members, can unite the team, enhance collegiality and collaboration which are indispensable for commitment, engagement, and high productivity.

It is normal for nursing personnel to scrutinize and analyze a leader's communication skills. Notes from *Voices from the nursing field* regarding some clinical leaders' communication include the following:

"She (the manager) is just plain awful, and lacks appropriate communication skills to lead this team. She speaks to us like we are children, often repeating herself over many times. She is always yelling. We hear her speaking from the north side of the department despite doors in between us. It is embarrassing for this profession to have such a leader. I never met a nursing officer who communicates so unprofessionally."

Remarkably, several nurses working at a university teaching hospital repeatedly voiced the following summary:

"She (the director) uses bullying communication style. She is the worse clinical leader in the system and is over five departments. It seems she comes up here to intimidate nurses, belittle us or make us understand she is the boss. Her managers communicate just like her. They speak disrespectfully to us, and it is not acceptable. That explains why nurses do not work in these departments for a long time. The turnover rate here is terrible. Nurses transfer out or leave after six months. Multiple complaints have been submitted to the Chief Nurse's office about her communication style but nothing has been done so far about it. They are trying to become a magnet hospital. I am not sure how they can achieve that status with this type of leadership behavior and nursing turnover. These nurses will not allow that to happen as we have one voice on this issue."

Other nurses said: "They have a girls' club of clinical leaders who have no respect for us nurses. The culture is to let the most unprofessional manager or nurse win more and have more power to talk down on us. She (the Director) was a nurse manager who spoke to staff in a very demeaning and non-supportive way. They made her the Director despite that. It seems to me they reward bad behavior, or make bad decisions. They replaced her with the loudest nurse who knows nothing, does not even have a BSN and cannot think for herself. She speaks like a street person and curses like a sailor. She needs to go back to school and learn how to communicate with adults, professionals, and in a work environment. They are all in the club. They all speak to staff in the same manner. She does not even know how to listen. She talks over everyone and rolls her eyes when nurses say something she does not like. She is the manager. Someone has to fix this."

There is not a defined list of things that clinical leaders or their representatives should communicate to clinical nurses. But there is a plethora of things that could be communicated to nurses in hospitals. However, regarding effective communication within the nursing team, nurses affirmed that they cared to know about the following important information:

The hospital's quality goals and their specific department's responsibilities in helping the hospital attain its goals, performance targets and benchmarks. A clinical department's quality goals may include a certain percentile ranking for patient satisfaction scores that would contribute to improve the hospital's overall scores on the Hospital Consumer Assessment of Healthcare Provider Systems (HCAPS) also known as the CAHPS reports. Clinical leaders are responsible for explaining what the HCAPS patient satisfaction scores entail, how many elements or measures the hospital is assessed on, and why it is important to score above other hospitals in their geographic area. Without clearly and unequivocally articulating the goals and performance targets, and staff's responsibilities in attaining the hospital's patient experience goals, achieving them could be more unlikely than the reverse. It is unfair to blame departmental nurses for poor performance on goals when they neither know what the goals and benchmarks are, nor have not been made to understand the part they play in achieving the goals. If the information is important to nurses, then share it with them.

All communication needs to be done in a timely manner. For example, several hospitals make it an important point for leaders to complete employees' performance evaluation timely and provide them feedback of any nature on time. Some hospital leaders omit completing and communicating this important piece of information with their staff until staff request it. Another example is when important organizational changes are planned, whether the changes will affect nursing staff or not, clinical leaders should share the information in a timely fashion with all members of the organization, so it is not transmitted through the grapevine, or "known by a selected few." Besides, employees need to understand why the changes are taking place or why the decision for the changes were made if it was not evident to employees.

Communication is a two-way process; therefore, leaders should listen attentively to staff during the communication process. Listening skills are an integral part of effective communication. Communication is incomplete if the leader does not receive confirmation of message receipt and comprehension of the subject matter by employees. Leaders should seek nurses' feedback after communicating with them or ask them for questions, suggestions, remarks or general feedback during the communication process

Effective communication is not always a walk in a park. Some people are naturally gifted communicators, others are not, and need or have to learn the skills of an effective communicator to successfully do it. To achieve effective communication in a culturally and generationally diverse group of individuals sounds like a challenge. It is important for hospital organizations to assist clinical leaders develop their communication skills when and where needed through training. Any improvement in communication skills for clinical leaders would better prepare and assist them in bridging the alleged gap in effective and respectful communication that is existing on their part toward professional nurses.

When communicating with nurses, clinical leaders should consider the following as a rule of thumb: Always, communication with staff should be in the official language of the organization even when the leader can speak a foreign language with some of the staff. To speak Spanish, Nigerian languages, Filipino, Hindi or Bengali on a nursing unit, in the presence of other team members is a demonstration of unprofessionalism. Leaders should not engage in their dialect with individuals with whom they share a common dialect. Leaders should clearly express their thoughts in a manner that avoids any potential discernment of ambiguity in their message.

When speaking with staff, clinical leaders should remain attentive to the staff member's body language, demonstrate appropriate listening techniques and ask questions of the staff to confirm their understanding of the message delivered. Being careful with personal body language is an important consideration for leaders when communicating with staff. At times, body language which is part of non-verbal communication could portray a completely different information than the intended message and information given verbally. When communicating with a subordinate, leaders should be sure to maintain eye contact with him or her. When speaking to multiple staff in a small group, share eye contact with each one of them by not focusing eye contact on one area, person or group if speaking with multiple staff members. However, when communicating on a one-on-one situation with staff, do not fail to maintain eye contact with the individual staff and use an appropriate tone of voice and body posture always.

Great leaders use motivating, qualitative and respectful interpersonal communication to develop powerful, trustworthy and long-lasting relationships with individual employees. Nurses are more prone to work with clinical leaders they trust, leaders who treat them as individual members of a team.

Question: Compare the two scenarios involving two different clinical leaders' communication style, and determine which one of them is an example of respectful and effective communication. On which team would you want to belong as a nurse and/or clinical leader? Explain your response.

Team I on Patient Experience:

"We are struggling as a unit on patient experience scores. Our target is a mean score of 90 and percentile ranking of 90. We did not meet our benchmark for the quarter. As a team, we are responsible for meeting our department's patient experience target each month and every quarter. We agreed as a team that this is our baby at work. We each represent this team. So, let us discuss possible reasons for missing our target and how we can move forward with confidence that together, we will achieve our goal next month and beyond. Who wants to start the discussion?"

Team II on Patient Experience:

"Y'all this is my unit and I am monitoring everything each one of you do. I have been monitoring you guys, and I know why I did not meet my patient satisfaction goal this quarter. I represent this unit and all Y'all do here. I must make sure my unit excels in patient satisfaction next month. I will not tolerate nurses not smiling with patients and answering call lights on time. I told you this last month, and here we are again with missed goals. This score must reach the goal if you want to work here. I hope I have made myself understood. Now let us get to work."

Team I on Fall Prevention Efforts:

"The number of patient falls on our night shift in this department is high. This is not representative of the hard work we do as a team to prevent our patients from falling. Remember what we say in this department: We are only as good as our patients' outcomes. We work hard and deserve better outcomes. What do you think is causing our patients to fall more frequently at night? Let us discuss possible strategies we can implement to reduce this issue so we can be happy with our contributions to keep our patients safe from the possible harm from fall."

Team II on Fall Prevention Efforts:

"Guys, the night shift fall rate is high. This is my unit and I will not tolerate patients falling at night. What do you all do on the night shift? You do not answer the call lights at night. That is why I am having this problem.

It is time to start writing up nurses when their patient falls. I will have your managers begin writing you up for patient's fall, or you tell me why I should not punish you for that."

The idea of effective communication by leaders such as in the team examples above may be stunningly different but they are real, borrowed from "voices from the nursing field." Effective and respectful communication with employees could be about myriad aspects of the job including specific achievable departmental goals, shared responsibilities for achieving the goals, performance targets or benchmarks, and the requirement for team effort and collaboration to achieve set goals, etcetera. Clinical leaders need to have communication skills that motivates nurses to collaborate with them, and that increases their desire to work harder for the collective success of the team.

Research indicates that when leaders let employees understand that they are an integral part of an organization and together they have a common goal, they are more likely to motivate and incite positive employee attitude toward work, and increase the potential for employee engagement. Besides, leaders should role model respectful and effective communication, thereby setting the pace for staff to improve their individual communication skills for the benefit of the team and the profession.

Transformational leaders use skilled communication to nurture their employees, build their self-esteem, empower and engage them (Bass). Leaders use motivating, qualitative and respectful interpersonal communication to develop powerful, trustworthy and long-lasting relationships with individual employees.

Nurses are more prone to work with clinical leaders they trust, leaders who treat them as individual members of a team.

Fair Pay – Money Matters

There exists an infinite body of literature opposing motivation strategies that include financial incentives. However, other authors support financial incentives as motivation techniques for workers' commitment. While researchers hold opposing perspectives regarding the use of money to incentivize employees, in nursing, the use of money as an incentive may be beneficial for plausible reasons.

Clinical nurses are neither bank nor company executives who receive scandalous amounts of money for incentive bonuses. Clinical nurses are not the bosses in hospitals. They are healthcare professionals who provide safe, quality care, treatment and services for the sick in different types of hospitals. Bedside nursing is a gratifying but tedious profession with uncountable ultra-high-level stressors. Some nurses work very long hours such as twelve-hour shifts, and the job is mentally and physically very taxing. While some hospital executives take home hefty amounts of money on incentive bonuses depending on the hospital's performance measures, some nurses do not receive a fair pay to incentivize them. It is important for clinical leaders to ascertain that their organizations compensate their nurses fairly across the board.

Perspectives echoed by several nurses during my enduring career in hospitals support the need to pay nurses fairly and very well, to incentive, motivate and prevent them from abandoning a profession many nurses say does not pay enough for the work it requires of them. In my collection of "Voices from the nursing field," more than 80 percent of the voices mentioned fair pay and money as a motivator. A nurse stated unequivocally:

"I would be engaged if I am well paid, or simply paid fairly. I am the supervisor for the department and have more experience than a colleague who is the charge nurse. This hospital hired us at around the same time, but she earns ten dollars an hour more than I. There is no good explanation for this. It is not motivating. I work at another hospital, and they pay me my worth. I prefer to work more there, and I feel more engaged there. These are two different hospitals in the same area. Why does X pay me so much less? And why does a charge nurse of lesser experience earn more money than I do? Their shift diffs are also poor. It does not motivate me. A nice and fair pay will motivate me. All the leaders get the big bonuses while some of us get whatever."

Several nurse voices contributed to the following, summarized in a paragraph:

"What about engagement? The best way to engage me is by paying fairly. Some of us are not well paid. It is impossible to feel engaged when you know that you are receiving less pay than the nurse working with you on the same shift, and there is not a reason why she should earn more. There are no incentive bonuses either. It would be great to look forward to a bonus every so often. The money would be my motivator. Sometimes I ask for a two-hundred-dollar bonus pay when they are short-staffed and ask for my help. That is my way to get the money I deserve. They are often short-staff, so I use those opportunities to work extra shifts and get the bonus pay. We all like fair and deserved pay. When they are very desperate, we ask for $300 bonus pay. Money helps get a lot done for me. If the hospital paid me well and fairly, I would be happy to fill in for my normal pay and zero bonus pay when we are short-staffed. But that is not happening and will not happen any time soon. I do my job regardless, but there is my motivation. It is difficult to feel motivated when you are not paid fairly."

Additionally, some travel nurses echoed similar opinions summarized as follows:

"Travel nursing pays a lot more money than staff nursing. Staff nurses earn less than their worth at some hospitals. Some of us have experienced both regular staff and travel nursing. Travel nursing helps me make good money, have fun and visit new places. It allows me a lot of freedom too. It is difficult to feel motivated in nursing when some leaders don't care about you; some hospitals pay peanuts compared to the work we do as nurses. It is a tough job, very stressful and emotional, but without the pay. Travel nursing gives me work, fun and more money than regular staff nursing. I am very motivated during my travel assignments because I am well paid for each assignment. When we do not want to renew a travel contract, before it is over, we happily look forward to the next assignment. The money is amazing and in some hospitals, you get a sincere thank you from the managers."

Every working person wants to be paid fairly. Leaders are responsible for making sure that employees receive fair pay. Even with high levels of intrinsic motivation, when an employee feels that his or her pay is not fair, the motivation level stays at a minimum. Fair pay and money matters to nurses according to results from the field. Motivation and engagement come with equitable and fair pay in nursing and in every employment situation.

Motivation is a multifaceted phenomenon with a host of strategies available for clinical leaders to use in motivating nurses, excite them, increase their perception of job satisfaction, gain their trust, and engagement. Several of the elements of motivation discussed above may be implemented as strategies for a successful nurse work environment. Whatever the choices for incentives or motivators may be, with the abundance of non-monetary and monetary motivation strategies available, clinical leaders need to create and sustain a motivating work environment for nurses. When employees are motivated, it becomes easier for them to feel enthused and work energetically. A motivated nurse workforce or team of nurses are less inclined to harbor turnover intents, abandon the profession, and more likely to be committed and engaged employees.

To prevent nurse attrition and increase satisfaction and engagement, hospital leaders need to create more appreciative, caring and motivational cultures that focus optimally on achievements, and what can be further accomplished, with more positive energy. Contemporary Nurse Executives and hospitals leaders must find pragmatic ways of motivating nurses, and sustaining motivated nursing work environments in which nurses can thrive in their respective organizations.

Questions: As a hospital leader or clinical leader, what do you do to promote or support nurses' quality of work life balance?

What are some of the strategies you or your clinical leaders use to motivate nurses, and demonstrate daily appreciation for them?

Connection

In the competitive environment of hospitals, leaders' have multiple challenging responsibilities. In addition to motivating employees in order to improve engagement, retention and efficiency, leaders need to develop interpersonal skills to adequately interact and connect with stakeholders. Bass affirmed that transformational leadership is influential, and engages employees in ways that transform their relationship. For the relationship between leaders and employees to be transforming, leaders need to connect with employees. Connection with employees can occur through a leader's demonstration of a sincere interest in their well-being, by caring to ask about their families and the things that matter most to them, what their passions are, what makes them tick, what they value, and why they do what they do. Connection and connecting with employees transcends surface-level communication, and approachable, caring, understanding, and personable leaders connect more easily with employees.

Transformational leaders connect with employees by acknowledging the need for individual identity, and utilize individualized consideration to understand each employee in a personal way that is motivating for employees. Leaders' connection with nurses is fundamental to establish an enduring relationship between both parties. Leaders can connect with nurses through several other means. By establishing a culture of safety and promoting open, honest, and respectful communication with nurses, leaders can connect with employees. In a culture of safety, when nurses feel safe to ask questions knowing they will receive honest answers, report concerns without the fear of retaliation, and report errors without the fear of punishment, they connect with leaders.

Connection between hospital leaders and nurses is significant in establishing trust for the leader. Yukl (2010) suggests that transformational leadership is highly correlated with trust in leaders. When a leader connects with employees, a serious professional relationship establishes, resulting in employees' admiration and trust in the leader. Employees enthusiasm, satisfaction, and energy levels at work increase with trustworthy and admirable leaders. Hospital, clinical and nursing leaders' connection with clinical nurses is fundamental to building solid relationships necessary to engage and retain nurses, and conquer the nursing shortage.

Rene Rodriguez summed communication that has the potential to build connections by explaining the interpersonal technique of listening, observation, validation and expanding, which she termed L.O.V.E. – Listen – Listening carefully and empathetically enables one to formulate more appropriate responses to staff questions and/or perspectives engenders stronger connections, versus talking more or not listening attentively or interrupting to respond quickly.

Observe – During interactions with staff, it is important for leaders to observe their body language, tone of voice, and other simple nonverbal cues that are likely to be missed without observation. The cues help provide a better understanding of people.

Validate – When communicating with staff, validation can be done in various ways – by nodding, leaning in with a smile, manifesting excitement or enthusiasm with words or actions that demonstrate to staff that you see them, hear them, know them, and understand them.

Expand – It is beneficial to expand on surface-level conversations that are void of the depth that makes them more meaningful. Get to know their passion, what makes them smile, what movies they like etc.

Question? Have you connected recently with the nursing staff? What makes some of the nursing staff tick? What are some of their passions?

Effective Leadership

Leader-Nurse Transforming HCOs

Researchers and leadership literature credit effective leaders with several prime leadership characteristics. In acute care hospitals, possessing superior leadership skills is indispensable for success. Besides, in the current "Pay for performance" environment, where quality indicators including patient experience scores and results are meticulously measured and openly reported by the Centers for Medicare and Medicaid Services (CMS) via the "hospital compare" portal, it is beneficial to have exemplary leadership skills. Hospitals are operating in highly competitive environments, and effective healthcare leaders capable of attracting, hiring and retaining highly knowledgeable and skilled nurses certainly maintain a competitive advantage over hospitals with mediocre leaders, and difficulties retaining skilled nurses.

Effective hospital leaders collaborate with their clinical teams to transform their organization. Excellent leaders support coaching, educating, mentoring and staff training for enhanced skills set, performance improvement, job satisfaction, increased morale and engagement (as illustrated in figure 14).

217

Effective hospital leaders understand that when employees are satisfied and engaged, they become more willing to dispense optimal efforts to satisfy the leader and accomplish the job above expectations. Performance above expectations reaps improved organizational productivity.

In hospitals, improved productivity may entail several things including but not limited to attaining optimal quality of care for clients, high patient experience scores or results, excellent physician satisfaction, increased patient visits and patient loyalty resulting from the optimal quality of patient care and satisfaction. Hospitals' profits and financial benefits are the ultimate results that stem from the above arguments.

The importance of effective leadership skills that motivate, satisfy and engage nurses in hospitals cannot be overemphasized. Nurses are the fulcrum of hospitals. Without their qualitative services, not only would patient-safety and quality of care suffer, the hospital's reputation and bottom line would suffer from a cascade of problems emanating from nursing issues. Bass affirmed that transformational leadership is influential, and engage employees in ways that transform their relationship and the organization. The results of this research support the relationship between transformational leaders and nurses' engagement in hospitals. Effective leader-nurse relationships are essential to conquer the continuous nursing shortage through leader-nurse connection, satisfaction, engagement and retention.

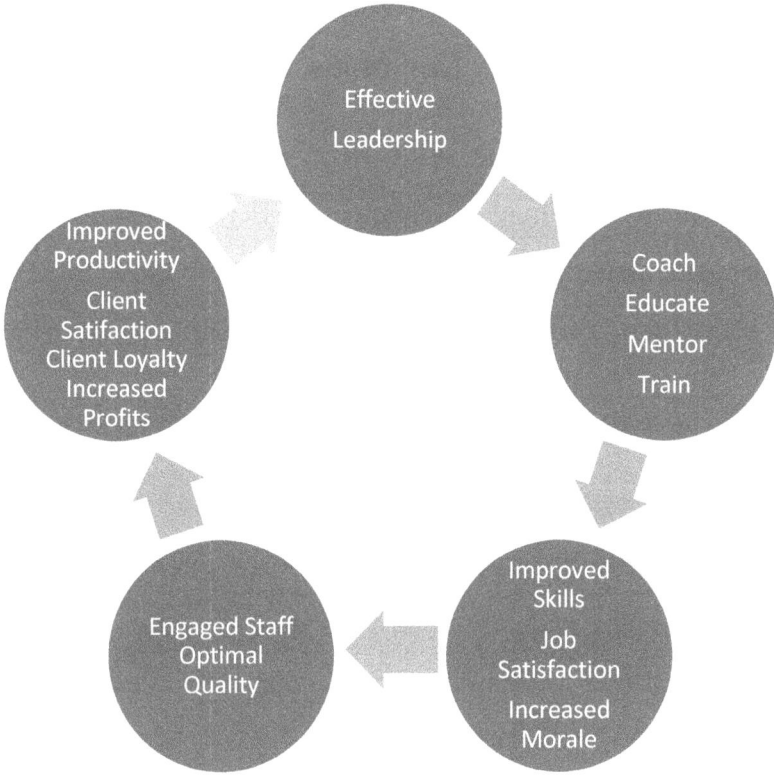

Fig. 14. Advantages of effective leaders: Leaders-nurses transforming relationship.

Human Resources Leadership Practice Essentials

Results of the study have paramount value for healthcare Human Resource (HR) professionals. Engagement is an integral part of the human resources component of healthcare administration. Human resource leaders should fundamentally address the problem of clinical nurses' engagement to minimize turnover and the intent to leave, dispel employee disengagement, increase satisfaction, retention, and commitment of keen employees, and therefore expand organizational profitability. Enhancing human efficiency and employee engagement have become serious subject matters for human resource executives due to the potential to maximize productivity and competitive advantage (Endres & Mancheno-Smoak, 2008).

A Calling

Many years ago bedside nursing was said to be a "calling." It was a profession for dedicated, selfless, caring and compassionate individuals who nursed the infirmed and the sick according to physician orders. While the care and compassion in nurses remain current, the profession is no longer a "calling." Currently for some, it is the fastest way of making money, while others say it guarantees a job, and yet others confirm they are in nursing "Just because their mom or sister or aunt is a nurse and that is just the professional choice for their family, not that they like to nurse sick people.

Devoid of "a personal calling to be a nurse", the inner desire and zeal for the profession coupled with the several challenges confronting nursing work environments including leadership problems, make it easy for nurse disengagement and attrition to be high. The role of human resources professionals is key in arresting the attrition and shortages in nursing, and in building and sustaining an engaged nursing workforce.

Selection of Clinical Leaders

It is commendable for healthcare organizations to develop future leaders through internal career paths and succession planning strategies. Professional growth from within an organization has several advantages, although it is not without shortcomings. In hospitals, often, the path to a clinical leadership position follows this trajectory:

Either highly skilled clinical nurses, a leader's pet, friend, relation of some sort, or a well-liked person often rise from a staff nurse position to a charge nurse role, then to a supervisory or lower management role.

Notwithstanding, some staff nurses have risen to clinical leadership roles without having an opportunity to supervise or manage first, and without basic knowledge or leadership skills. Active participation of human resource leaders in the internal promotion or hiring of clinical leaders is fundamental in placing the right leader with the appropriate clinical team.

Possession of great nursing knowledge, technical skills, and dexterity on the field do not necessarily translate to the potential of being a good clinical manager or leader responsible for either managing staff and departmental operations, or leading a team effectively to accomplish the strategic organizational goals or mission. While leadership skills are natural to some, for others, it has to be learned and practiced for proficiency. Given the complex roles and responsibilities clinical leaders currently assume in hospitals, it is a disservice to the nursing team, the department, the communities served, and the organization to promote nurses to leadership positions without equipping them for success with adequate education, coaching, and mentoring in effective leadership behaviors and skills.

Hospital HR leaders are responsible for asking the hard but right questions regarding the promotion of patient care nurses to clinical leadership roles because supreme practical nursing skills are neither equivalent to, nor a pre-requisite for effective clinical leadership skills.

In 2010, the Robert Wood Foundation Initiative on the Future of Nursing at the Institute Of Medicine (IOM) held three public forums in an effort to assess the challenges and opportunities in the nursing profession. One of the forums examined nursing education regarding what to teach, how to teach and where to teach nursing, to meet the workforce challenges. In addition to this effort, the IOM should consider the education of transformational clinical leaders and mentorships for acquiring effective leadership skills that empower nurses and prevent nurse attrition and the nurse shortage. Poor leadership skills are detrimental to nurses' retention, job satisfaction and nurse engagement.

Clinical leadership positions should have educational requirements that should be given serious considerations to recruit knowledgeable and competent clinical nurse leaders. A few years ago, several hospitals in the nation began requiring clinical leadership applicants to have a minimum education of Master's degree in Health Sciences, Nursing Science, Health Administration, Business Administration or Master's degree a healthcare related field. Individuals without a Master's degree who were already in clinical leadership positions before the trend started, were given the opportunity to further their education and enhance their knowledge base, skills and competency to remain in the role. Superior educational levels are fundamental in leadership positions and for effective leadership. Upholding this requirement is important in clinical leadership where competent leaders are needed to nurture, coach, empower, motivate and engage nurses.

Nurses that are interested in leadership posts need to prepare for clinical leadership roles and responsibilities through education and training. The HR department or its professionals are responsible for creating opportunities to train and develop effective leadership skills in nurses who chose the leadership path without having a formal education, or who become clinical leaders because of situational factors. They need to work in collaboration with senior nurse leaders of the organization to accomplish this.

Hospital HR leaders working in collaboration with clinical leadership teams are responsible for identifying nurses with a minimum education of Bachelor of Science in Nursing degree who possess leadership characteristics. Such nurses should be developed through further education, mentorship, and training for effectiveness in the leadership role. Besides, prior to considering their candidacy for a clinical leadership position, HR leaders should understand each nurse's individual motivations for leaving patient-care for a leadership role. HR leaders' identification of candidates' motivations that are related to the organizational culture, or to assist the growth and empowerment of other nurses are important considerations for clinical leader role selection.

HCO supported by a strong human resource department should have a professional development team that invests in developing transformational leaders in nursing. The results of this research clearly indicate that to a high degree; nursing engagement correlates with transformational leadership. Given the multiple challenges facing hospital leaders and the nursing attrition and shortage, hospital human resource professionals should seriously consider and encourage utilizing transformational leadership practices to engage nurses. The four characteristics of transformational leadership have manifested themselves in this research as highly desirable leadership qualities by clinical nurses. Nursing needs dynamic, motivated, uplifted, enthusiastic, and fair leaders, dedicated to assisting clinical nurses perform above and beyond to accomplish the hospital's mission and the departmental and individual professional goals.

Shared Values

Understanding the operational values of the organization they represent; Hospital HR leaders should develop and implement leadership interview questions that center on clinical leadership candidates' core values. Alexander (2006) asserts that the ability to identify, articulate and implement values provides a solid foundation of how a leader acts and the extent to which he or she may want to lead. An insight into the values of a candidate for clinical leadership by an interviewing HR

Director could be a determining factor in the hiring decision.

Lee & King explain in their well written 2001 guide that core values are the most vital concepts that individuals use for decision-making and to determine when, how and to what extent to act. Responses to interview questions that dig deeper into the beliefs and values of clinical leadership candidates would be indicative of their potential fit or incompatibility with the nursing or organizational values already established or in progress. Understanding the core values of an individual can be powerful in hiring decision-making processes because each person's core values provide insights into who they are and their potential to lead effectively, or fail at leadership, or be a misfit to the organization's nursing staff engagement endeavor.

Leadership candidates should answer questions that define their core values, identify the last time they did something significant that aligned with their core values, explaining how that looked like, what it meant and how it felt. Responses to core value-related questions could tell some of the candidate's story of who they are, and how and why they are a leader for a particular institution or not, because values influence behaviors and decisions.

Literature indicates that companies that define and place emphasis on their values are successful. Such organizations understand that employees' perception of individual values and organization's values is a determinant of job satisfaction and engagement.

The question recommended for HR professionals is the following: How do you define the relationship of clinical nurses' work engagement to the shared values between nurses and clinical leaders and the organization?

Emotional Intelligence

Emotional Intelligence (EI) in the context of this book, for clinical leaders, is their ability to understand their emotions while at work, and those of the individual staff members of their team, and to exert emotional self-control in order to appropriately manage their relationships. EI has four domains which clinical managers need to be aware of and they are namely: Self-awareness, self-management, social awareness, and relationship management. Leaders with supreme EI are needed in hospitals where emotions often run high in the operationally fast and stressful environments. Hospital HR leaders should build a clinical leadership toolkit that is loaded with huge amounts of EI. For decades now, because of little or no consideration for EI, communication patterns in some clinical environments remain problematic from many standpoints such as between physicians and nurses, among nurses, and between leaders, managers, and their subordinates.

Researchers posit that leaders who have superior skills in Emotional Intelligence can reduce the degree of defensive communication in hospitals organizations. Selecting leaders with high levels of EI would be beneficial to hospital organizations. Clinical leaders who can handle not only the emotional side of staff but also patients and families, can build energized and engaged employees, currently needed in acute care hospitals.

In *How healthcare leaders can increase emotional intelligence,* Scott reported the assertion of several theorists that successful healthcare leaders have the soft skills required to positively influence stakeholders. Demonstrating empathy toward employees, enhancing group and interpersonal relationships, and acknowledging the personal contributions of individual healthcare team members are some of the soft skills shared by Scott in his 2013 article on how to increase emotional intelligence in healthcare leaders.

EI is a skill that can be learned. Hence, new and inexperienced clinical leaders or clinical leaders with opportunities to improve personal emotional intelligence can learn the skill. According to Scott (2013), professional development efforts by HR leaders should consider the four skills that will assist in improving leaders' emotional intelligence, and the skills include: Self-awareness, self-management, social management, and relationship management. Being self-aware makes it easier to self-manage or control personal emotions. A leader who is aware of his or her personal emotions and manages them effectively would better manage social interactions and relationship with employees and other stakeholders. EI is critical to a leaders' success and effectiveness. HR leaders should attract, hire and retain emotionally intelligent clinical leaders to foster a culture of respectful communication and interactions in the hospital environments of care.

Responsibility and Accountability

The nursing shortage affects hospitals and healthcare consumers in multiple negative ways. There is a need for a serious Human Resources leader-led strategy to respond to the enduring nursing attrition and shortage to meet the changing healthcare landscape and the demands of healthcare consumers.

HR leaders are responsible for paying honest attention to expressed concerns and complaints by nurses and nurse managers about clinical leaders who do not model acceptable, professional behaviors and core values that are in sync with organizational culture. HR leaders need to be morally upright in this regard and be honest brokers for all their organization's human capital. It is unnecessary for HR leaders that are serious about curtailing the nurse turnover, attrition and shortage to cover-up complaints regarding unprofessional, bullying and inappropriate behaviors of some leaders towards nurses who are subordinates. Problem-solving by HR professionals include appropriately challenging leadership behaviors and attitudes that are not conducive to enhancing clinical nurses' engagement.

Hospital HR leaders are responsible for conscientiously and impartially assisting their organizations strategic human capital goals and sustaining morally correct organizational culture. The need for leaders' performance improvement in leadership style should be assessed, identified and acknowledged through the HR department from formal complaints submitted to the HR department by nurses and nurse managers. The responsibilities of HR leaders include holding clinical leaders accountable for their departments' turnover rates, their employee satisfaction levels, and nursing personnel engagement levels. HR leaders ensure clinical leaders are accountable not only for their departments' performance on human resources quality, but also for propagating values that have negative effects on nursing engagement, and for bedside nursing turnover rates and attrition.

The establishment, sustainability, and standardization of processes and strategies that support nurses' work environments rests upon the shoulders of hospital HR leaders. They need to initiate the creation and evolution of clinical leadership practices to incorporate leadership styles that are desirable for nursing work environments. The ultimate objective for HR strategies to improve clinical leadership practices should be grounded in stopping nursing attrition, increasing nurse retention, job satisfaction and nurse engagement, with the end result of optimal quality of patient care and safety.

The job of clinical nurses centers mostly around duties performed to fundamentally improve the health and well-being of patients which needs engaged performance. Working short-handed, serving the ailing in a stressful, fast-paced environment with passive-avoidant, laissez-faire and solely transactional leaders who manage by exception, is not a recipe for improving nursing engagement. Work environments that are devoid of employee engagement make it hard for nurses to dispense safe care for the ultimate improvement of consumer's well-being.

Hospital HR leaders could build an organizational guide for hiring and retaining quality nurses, for assessing and identifying individual and collective nursing needs for job satisfaction, commitment, and engagement. Establish a pyramid with prioritized nurse engagement needs and make active efforts to hire clinical leaders who share the hospital's values, appreciate and understand nurses' needs. Such a plan can be accomplished by utilizing input from nurses on professional forums and discussion boards and other professional platforms and forums. It is always important to include the perspectives of the professionals whose work engagement strategy is the focus of the agenda in order to obtain success in the effort.

Accept the Realities and Take Action

Despite the shortages in nursing, hospital leaders should learn to accept the realities of the presence of disengaged and actively disengages nurses among patient-care staff, and take action accordingly irrespective of the causes of the disengagement. Lack of intrinsic motivation to perform a job cannot be changed using external motivators no matter how exciting the extrinsic elements of motivation are. While there are no guarantees that disengaged nurses may become engaged employees, there is a possibility to move from disengagement to engagement. On the other hand, it is impossible for actively disengaged nurses to become engaged employees.

Engaged nurses are high performers, highly productive employees whose cost to the organization is low. Engaged nurses arrive at work early or on time, are energetic, enthusiastically ready for work, and perform more than expected, and rarely make costly errors. Engaged nurses are highly focused, participate in risk identification and mitigation, and proactively resolve patient care concerns through timely service recovery. They are active participants in team and departmental performance improvement projects, hospital taskforce committee work, respond timely to patients' needs and help build or manage-up team members.

Conversely, actively disengaged nurses are costly to hospitals. They often have high level of absenteeism, are usually late for their shift, have a high potential to make costly errors, and potentially discourage disengaged employees. They could be the Debbie Downers of the team, and could slowly pull disengaged staff to the actively disengaged state. Actively disengaged nurses are low performers who do not want to belong to the team, and they are not motivated. Actively disengaged nurses' productivity level is often minimal (as illustrated on figure 15).

Cost and Productivity Equation

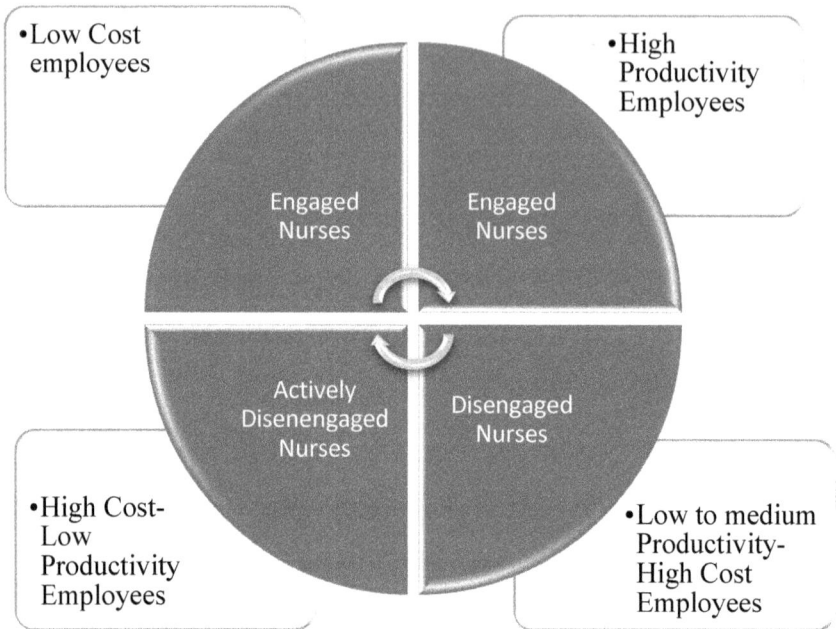

•Low Cost employees

•High Productivity Employees

Engaged Nurses

Engaged Nurses

Actively Disenengaged Nurses

Disengaged Nurses

•High Cost- Low Productivity Employees

•Low to medium Productivity- High Cost Employees

Fig. 15. Cost and productivity in the equation

Disengaged nurses could become engaged employees with the use of external motivators. They float in-between the actively disengaged and engaged nurses regarding cost and are medium performers regarding productivity. Actively disengaged and disengaged nurses are mediocre performers but are costly to hospitals.

HR Directors need to analyze the performance of such nurses and be ready to accept hard facts that suggest they are negatively affecting the clinical team and the hospital.

Nursing shortage does not mean that mediocre performance and low performing, unmotivated nurses should be tolerated in hospitals. When it is evident that all reasonable efforts to motivate disengaged nurses for engagement are futile, and when nurses are evidently actively disengaged and represent risks for patient safety and peer engagement, it is time for HR leaders to help transition them to a different job specification, department, or completely out of the organization through termination as the situation may warrant. Holding onto underperforming, unmotivated, disengaged nurses poses a high patient safety and organizational risk in several ways.

Engaged, Disengaged, and Actively Disengaged Nurses are Worlds Apart on Cost and Productivity.

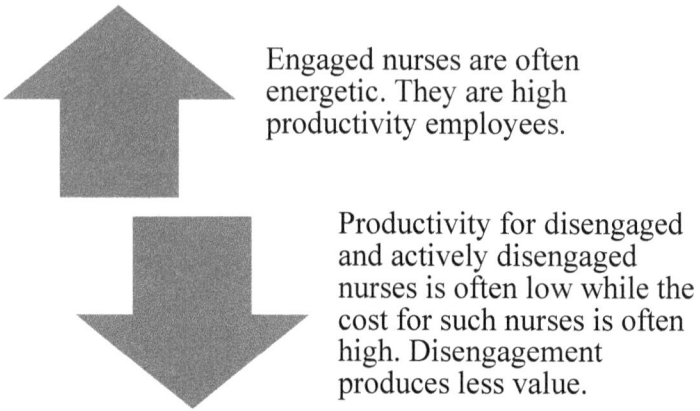

Engaged nurses are often energetic. They are high productivity employees.

Productivity for disengaged and actively disengaged nurses is often low while the cost for such nurses is often high. Disengagement produces less value.

Fig. 16. Cost, Productivity and Performance of engaged, disengaged and actively disengaged nurses.

Gauging Nurses' Engagement

HR professionals must demonstrate active involvement in the healthcare community's attempts to combat and conquer the nursing shortage. Monitoring clinical staff's response to HR departmental efforts to maintain a positive morale is key to effective HR management. A practical strategy for gauging employee morale and the level of clinical staff's engagement is to administer employee engagement surveys. Engagement surveys are a credible means to sought employees' feedback and understand their perspectives about their leaders, the organization, and their level of engagement in the organizational mission.

Results of the surveys should be discussed with leaders and used to the organization's operational benefits. Identified trends toward a downward slope of employee engagement should be a signal that attentiveness is required in the area of employee morale and the level of engagement. Failing engagement scores or a consistent drop in the scores should prompt an immediate plan of action by HR professionals in collaboration with nurse leaders and executives to remediate the situation.

Training Future Leaders

Hospital HR directors reserve the ultimate responsibility to recruit, train and develop more transformation clinical nurse leaders to lead nursing departments satisfactorily, reduce the rate of nursing turnover, and curb the shortfall. To assist in conquering the nursing shortage, HR leaders in contemporary healthcare organization need to be more astute in their strategies to curb clinical nurses' dissatisfaction, attrition, and turnover rates. The preparation of future nurse leaders needs focus on training younger managers who seek career progression to take on transformational leadership roles. Results from this study indicated that male and female employees experienced higher levels of employee engagement when the leader exhibited more transformational behaviors. Additionally, the youngest poll of nurses in the current research (18 to 31 years old) experienced a higher degree of engagement when transformational leadership style was used by clinical leaders. Given that the nursing workforce is currently made up of more younger clinicians after the retirement of many baby boomers, HR professionals should prepare a strategy for training younger leaders to take on transformational leadership roles in healthcare organizations.

The Case for Transformational Clinical Leaders

Employees who feel happy at work are more liable to be engaged in the organizational mission than employees who feel frustrated and disenchanted. According to Syndell (2008), transformational leaders possessed a scientific approach to leadership with a humanistic style of management that produces happy self-actualized employees. Hospital leaders are still confronted with challenges of clinical nursing shortages, turnover and a value-based system that can align organizational goals with engaged employees. Healthcare organizational leaders have not proffered standard solutions to hospital problems related to clinical nursing turnover, work unit shortages and values.

The research findings significantly contributed to the existing knowledge-based related to leadership styles that foster employee engagement for clinical nurses in healthcare organizations.

Per bass (1997), transformational leadership is considered effective in any situation or organizational culture. Yukl (2010) affirms that the theory does not specify situations where transformational leadership is irrelevant or ineffective. To support this assertion, the positive relationship between transformational leadership and effectiveness has been reproduced for leaders at various levels of authority, in diverse types of organizations, and in many countries (Bass, 1997). With the need for a leadership style that would help motivate nurses, arrest the nursing attrition, and enhance nurse engagement in hospitals, this research findings indicate that nurses' engagement correlates with transformational leadership.

The Nutshell of Nurse Engagement

Nurse Engagement Benefits in a Nutshell

Clinical nursing employee engagement is critical to the provision of high-quality patient care, as well as to improving the organizations financial capabilities. HR directors have the responsibility and legitimate power to help healthcare organizations ensure that clinical nursing staff engagement remains a viable strategy for effectively managing human and financial resources in hospitals.

The benefits of nursing engagement in a hospital's Mission are multifold (as illustrated on figure 17). The advantages of having an engaged clinical nurse workforce are innumerable and this book discusses them at length. Hospital executives and leaders may dissect the book to establish the long list of what is possible for their organizations when their nurses are committed and engaged.

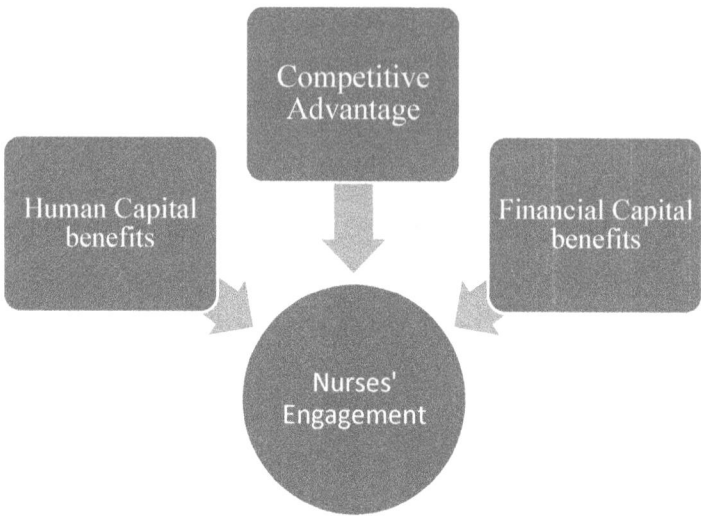

Fig. 17. Nurses' Engagement Benefits in a Nutshell

Conclusion

In the contemporary organizational environments of the 21st century, effective leadership is required for healthcare organizations to meet or exceed their goals and hence succeed in the industry.

This book contributes to the current body of knowledge regarding leadership and employee engagement in varied ways. The research results the provide the foundation of the book provided empirical evidence that transformational and transactional leadership patterns are positively related to clinical nurses' engagement behaviors. Empirical evidence obtained from data analysis validated the theory that transformational leadership is a better predictor of engagement due to its higher level of correlation with perceived engagement behaviors of clinical nurses as compared to transactional leadership. The results and conclusions underscore the importance of leadership styles in relation to clinical nurses' engagement levels in hospital organizations.

With the enduring nursing shortages in hospitals across America, it is fundamental for healthcare leaders to utilize motivational strategies to engage nurses in their hospital's mission, beat attrition and turnover rates and conquer the shortages in one hospital at a time. "One hospital at a time", beginning with your organization.

INDEX

T

REFERENCES

Adams, L. T. (2009). *Nursing shortage solutions and America's economic recovery, Nursing Education Perspectives,* 30(6), 349. Retrieved December 10, 2009. From EBSCOhost

Aiken, L. H., Clarke, S. P., Sloan, D. M., Sochalski, J., & Silber, J. H. (2002). Hospital nurse staffing and patient mortality, nurse burnout, and job dissatisfaction. *Journal of the American Medical Association, 288*(16), 1987-1993. Retrieved December 12, 2009 Nursing@Ovid

American Association of Colleges of Nursing. (2008). Nursing shortage fact sheet. Retrieved February 26, 2010 from ProQuest.

American Nurses Association (2008). *What is the magnet recognition program?* Retrieved February 24, 2010, from http://nursecredentialing.org/magnet/

American Nurses Association. (2010a). National nursing shortage facts. Retrieved February

26, 2010 from

http://ftp.hrsa.gov/bhpr/workforce/behindshorta
ge.pdf

American Nurses Association. (2010b). Occupational
employment. Retrieved February 26, 2010 from
http://www.bls.gov/opub/ooq/2007/fall/art02.p
df

American Hospital Association. (2006-2010). Research
and trends. Retrieved February 26, 2010 from
http://www.aha.org/aha/research-and-
trends/index.html

Anand, S. (1997). Leadership: The manager v. the leader.
IIE Solutions, 29(9), 34-35. Retrieved November
2010, from EBSCOhost.

Atchinson, T. A. & Carlson, G. (2009). *Leading healthcare
cultures: How human capital drives financial performance.*
Chicago, IL: Health Administration Press.

Avolio, B. (1999). *Full leadership development.* Thousand
Oaks, CA: Sage.

Avolio, B. J., Bass, M. B. and Jung, D. I. (1999) Re-
examining the components of transformational and
transactional leadership using the Multifactor
Leadership Questionnaire, *Journal of Occupational and*

Organizational Psychology, 72(4), 441-463. Retrieved January 18, 2010, from EBSCOhost.

Avolio, B. J. & Yammarino, F. J. (2002). *Transformational and charismatic leadership: The road ahead.* San Diego, CA: Emerald.

Avolio, B. J. & Yammarino, F. J. (2008). *Transformational and charismatic leadership: The road ahead.* Bingley, UK: Emerald Group Publishing Limited.

Bakker, A. B., Schaufeli, W. B., Leiter, M. P., & Taris, T. W. (2008). Work engagement: An emerging concept in occupational health psychology. *Work and Stress, 22*(3), 187-22. Retrieved February 11, 2010 from EBSCOhost.

Barnard, C. (1936). *The functions of the executive.* Cambridge, MA: Harvard University Press.

Bass, B. (1985). *Leadership and performance beyond expectations.* New York: The Free Press.

Bass, B. (1990). *Bass & Stogdill's handbook of leadership theory, research, and managerial application.* New York, NY: Free Press.

Bass, B. M. (1999). Two decades of research and development in transformational leadership. *European Journal of Work and Organizational Psychology,*

8(1), 9-32. Retrieved November 25, 2010, from EBSCOhost.

Bass, B. M., & Avolio, B. J. (1990). The implications of transactional and transformational leadership for individual, team, and organizational development. *Research in Organizational Change and Development, 4,* 231-272. Retrieved March 25, 2010 from EBSCOhost.

Bass, B. M., & Avolio, B. J. (1995). *1995 Sample Multifactor Leadership Questionnaire technical report.* Redwood City, CA: Mind Garden, Inc.

Bass, B. M. & Avolio, B. J. (2004). *Multifactor Leadership Questionnaire Third edition manual and sampler set.* Redwood City, CA: Mind Garden, Inc.

Bass, B. M., Avolio, B. J., Jung, D. I., & Berson, Y. (2003). Predicting unit performance by assessing transformational and transactional leadership. *Journal of Applied Psychology, 88*(2), 207-218. Retrieved November 25, 2010, from EBSCOhost.

Bass, B. M., & Riggio, R. E. (2006). *Transformational leadership.* Mahwah, NJ: Erlbaum.

Bennis, W. (1999). The end of leadership: Exemplary leadership is impossible without full inclusion, initiatives, and cooperation of followers. *Organizational Dynamics, 28*(1), 71-80. Retrieved November 16, 2010, from EBSCOhost.

Bielski, L. (2006). Outsourcing success. It's all in the governance. *ABA Banking Journal 98, 7*(38), 40-42. Retrieved November 16, 2010 from ProQuest Business.

Blausten, P. (2009). Keep your focus on engagement. *Human Resources,* 22-22. Retrieved   October 26, 2010, from EBSCOhost.

Boje, D. (2003). Transformational leadership. Retrieved October 26, 2010, from http://cbae.nmsu.edu/~dboje/teaching/338/trans formational_leadership.htm#bass.

Boerner, S., Eisenbeiss, S. A., & Griesser, D. (2007). Follower behavior and organizational performance: The impact of transformational leaders. *Journal of Leadership & Organizational Studies, 13*(3), 15-26. Retrieved May 3, 2014, from EBSCOhost.

Bones, C. (2007). Engagement is at the heart of M & A. *Ivey Business Journal. 71*(3),1. Retrieved from on February 12, 2011 from EBSCOhost.

Borrego, M., Douglas, E. P., & Amelink, C. T. (2009). Quantitative, qualitative, and mixed research methods in engineering education. *Journal of Engineering Education, 98*(1), 53-66. Retrieved June 10, 2012 from ProQuest.

Brace, N., Kemp, R., & Snelgar, R. (2006). *SPSS for psychologists* (3rd ed.). Mahwah, NJ: Lawrence Erlbaum Associates, Publisher.

Broom, M. (2003). Positive use of power. *Executive Excellence, 20*(2), 11. Retrieved December 12, 2010 from EbscoHost.

Brymer, E., & Gray, T. (2006). Effective leadership: Transformational or transactional? *Australian Journal of Outdoor Education. Milton, 10*(2), 13-19. Retrieved March 14, 2010 from Google scholar.

Burns, J. M. (1978). *Leadership.* New York, NY: Harper & Row.

Buerhaus, P., Auerbach, D., & Staiger, D. O. (2007). Recent trends in the registered labor market in the U.S.: Short-run swings on top of long-term trends. Nursing Economics, *25*(2), 59. Retrieved February 26, 2010, from ProQuest.

Buerhaus, P. I., Donelan, K., Ulrich, B. T., Norma, L., Desroches, C., & Dittus, R. (2007). Impact of the nurse shortage on hospital patient care: Comparative perspectives. *Health Affairs, 26,* 853-862. Retrieved November 24, 2010 from EBSCOhost.

Buckingham, M., & Coffman, C. (1999). *First break all the rules.* New York, NY: Simon & Schuster.

Castellari, C. M. (2010). Quantitative and qualitative research: A view for clarity. *International Journal of Education,* 2(2), 1-14. Retrieved June 6, 2012 from Proquest.

Catteeuw, F., Flynn, E., & Vonderhorst, J. (2007). Employee engagement: Boosting productivity in turbulent times. *Organization Development Journal,* *25*(2), 151-157. Retrieved March 16, 2011, from EBSCOhost.

Christensen, L. B., Johnson, R. B., & Turner, L. A. (2011). *Research methods, design, and analysis.* Noston, MA: Allyn & Bacon.

Clawson, J. G. (2006). *Level three leadership: Getting below the surface.* Upper Saddle River, NJ: Pearson.

Cleary, M., & Hunt, G. E. (2010). Building community engagement in nursing. *The Journal of Continuing Education in Nursing,* 41(8), 344-5. Retrieved February 21, 2011 from ProQuest Health and Medicine.

Cohen, J. (1988). *Statistical power analysis for the behavioral sciences* (2nd ed.). St. Paul, MN: West Publishing Company. Cohen, J., Cohen, P., West, S. G., & Aiken, L. S. (2003). *Applied multiple regression/correlation analysis for the behavioral sciences* (3rd Ed). Mahwah, NJ: Lawrence Erlbaum Associates.

Cook, J., Hepworth, S., Wall, T., & Warr, P. (1989). *The experience of work: A compendium and review of 249 measures and their use.* New York, NY: Academic Press.

Cooper, D., & Schindler, P. (2003). *Business research methods.* New York, NY: McGraw-Hill.

Crabtree, S. (2005). Engagement keeps the doctor away. *Gallup Management Journal Online,* 1-4. Retrieved November 22, 2010, from EBSCOhost.

Creswell, J. W. (2005). *Educational research planning, conducting, and evaluating quantitative and qualitative research*. Upper Saddle River, NJ: Pearson.

Creswell, J. W. (2008). Research design: Qualitative, quantitative and mixed methods approaches. Thousand Oaks, CA: Sage Publications.

Demerouti, E. & Bakker, A. B. (2008). The Oldenburg Burnout Inventory: A good alternative to measure burnout and engagement. In J.R.B. Halbesleben (Ed.), Handbook of stress and burnout in healthcare. Hauppauge, NY: Nova Science.

Devane, D., Begley, C., & Clark, M. (2004). How many do I need? Basic principles of sample size estimation. *Journal of Advanced Nursing, 47*(3), 297-302. doi: 10.1111/j.1365-2648.2004.03093.x

DeVellis, R. F. (2012). *Scale development: Theory and applications* (3rd ed.). Thousand Oaks, CA: Sage Publications.

Donley, R. (2005). Challenges for nursing in the 21st century. *Nursing Economics, 23*(6), 312-318. Retrieved April 24, 2009 from ProQuest health & medicine.

Drucker, P. (2004). *The post-capitalist society*. Burlington, MA: Butterworth-Heinemann.

Elster, R., & Corral, T. (2009). Leaders forging values-based change: Partnership power for the 21st century. *Beliefs & Values, 1*(1), 31-44. *Springer Publishing Company*. Retrieved March 28, 2009, from EBSCOhost.

Elgie, R. (2007). Politics, economics, and nursing shortages: A critical look at United States Government Policies. *Nursing Economics, 25*(5), 285–292. Retrieved December 20, 2010 from EBSCOhost.

Ellefsen, B. & Kim, H. S. (2005). Nurses' clinical engagement: A study from an acute-care setting in Norway. *Research and Theory for Nursing Practice,19*(4), 297-313. Retrieved February 12, 2011 from ProQuest health and medicine.

Endres, G. M., & Mancheno-Smoak, L. (2008). The human resource craze: Human performance improvement and employee engagement. *Organization Development Journal, 26*(1), 69-78. Retrieved December 10, 2010, from EBSCOhost.

Faul, F., Erdfelder, E., Lang, A. G., & Buchner, A. (2007). G*Power 3: A flexible statistical power analysis for the social, behavioral, and biomedical sciences. *Behavior Research Methods, 39*(2), 175-191. doi: 10.3758/BF03193146

Ferguson, L. (2004). External validity, generalizability, and knowledge utilization. *Journal of Nursing Scholarship, 36*(1), 16-22. doi: 10.1111/j.1547-5069.2004.04006.x

Fernandez, C. P. (2007). Employée engagement. *Journal of Public Health Management and Practice, 13*(5), 524-526. Retrieved May 18, 2010, from Nursing@Ovid.

Fisher, C., Schoenfeldt, L., & Shaw, J. (2006). *Human resource management.* Boston, MA: Houghton Mifflin.

Fiedler, F.E. (1967). *A theory of leadership effectiveness.* New York, NY: McGraw-Hill.

Fitzpatrick, M. A. (2000). What are your rules of engagement? *Nursing Management,* 13(8), 6. Retrieved February 12, 2011 from ProQuest Health and Medicine.

Fox, A. (2010). Raising engagement. *HR Magazine, 55*(5), 34-40. Retrieved February 12, 2011 from ProQuest

Fowler, D. L. (2014). Career Coaching: Innovative Academic--Practice Partnership for Professional Development. The Journal of Continuing Education in Nursing, 45(5), 205—209.

Fox, R. L. & Abrahamson, K. (2009). A Critical examination of the U.S. nursing shortage: Contributing factors, public policy implications. *Nursing Forum, 44*(4), 235-244. Retrieved March 10, from ProQuest.

Frank, F., Finnegan, D., Richard, P., & Taylor, C. R. (2004). The race for talent: Retaining and engaging workers in the 21st century. *Human Resource Planning, 27*(3), 12-25. Retrieved November 22, 2010, from EBSCOhost.

Frese, M. (2008). The word is out: We need an active performance concept for modern workplaces. *Industrial and Organizational Psychology, 1*(1), 67–69. Retrieved March 28, 2009, from EBSCOhost.

Fried, B. J. & Frottler, M. D. (Eds.). (2008). *Human resources in healthcare: Managing for success.* Health Administration Press.

Gallup, G. (2009). The relationship between engagement at work and organizational outcome. Retrieved October 20, 2010, from googlescholar.

Garner, J. W. (2000). The nature of leadership. In *The Jossey-Bass reader on educational leadership*. San Francisco: Jossey-Bass.

Gilkey, R. W. (Ed.). (1999). *The 21st century health care leader*. San Francisco, CA: Jossey-Bass.

George, D. & Mallery, P. (2010). *SPSS for Windows step by step: a simple guide and* Reference, 18.0 update (11th ed.). Boston, MA: Allyn and Bacon.

Goffee, R., & Jones, G. (2000). Why should anyone be led by you? *Harvard Business Review, 78*(5), 62-70. Retrieved October 16, 2010 from EBSCOhost.

Goldfarb, M. G., Goldfarb, R. S., & Long, M. C. (2008). Making sense of competing nursing shortage concepts. *Policy, Politics & Nursing Practice, 9*(3), 192–202. Retrieved October 22, 2010 from Nursing@Ovid.

Grealish, L. (2000). The skills of coach are an essential element in clinical learning. Journal of Nursing Education, 39(5), 231-233.

Golman, D. (2002). Primal leadership: Realizing the
power of emotional intelligence. *Personnel Psychology,
55*, 1030-1033. Retrieved October 12, 2010 from
Gale power search.

Guo, S., & Hussey, D. L. (2004). Non-probability
sampling in social work research: Dilemmas,
consequences, and strategies. *Journal of Social Service
Research, 30*(3), 1-18. doi:10.1300/J079v30n03_01

Harter, J. K., Schmidt, F. L., & Hayes, T. L. (2002).
Business-unit-level relationship between employee
satisfaction, employee engagement, and business
outcomes: A meta-analysis. *Journal of Applied
Psychology, 87*(2), 268-279. Retrieved October 12,
2010, from EBSCOhost.

Haq, I. U., Ali, A., Azeem, M. U., Hijazi, S. T., Qurashi,
T. M., & Quyyum, A. (2010). Mediation role of
employee engagement in creative work process on
the relationship of transformational leadership and
employee creativity. *European Journal of Economics,
Finance and Administrative Sciences, 25*, 94-101.
Retrieved February 6, 2011 from EBSCOhost.

Heffes, E. M. (2003). Energy the currency of personal productivity. *Financial Executive, 19*(7), 39-41. Retrieved January 11, 2010, from EBSCOhost.

Heger, B. (2007). Linking the employee value proposition (EVP) to employee engagement and business outcomes: Preliminary findings from a linkage research pilot study. *Organization Development Journal Chesterland, 25*(2), 121-134. Retrieved April 9, 2008, from ProQuest.

Heifetz, R., & Laurie, D. (2001). The work of leadership. *Harvard Business Review, 79*(11), 131-141. Retrieved February 6, 2010, from EBSCOhost.

Heller, F. A. (1973). Leadership, decision-making, and contingency theory. *Industrial Relations, 12*(2), 183-199. Retrieved October 20, 2010, from EBSCOhost.

Hemp, P. (2008). Where will we find tomorrow's leaders? *Harvard Business Review, 86* (1), 123-129. Retrieved November 16, 2010, from EBSCOhost.

Hersey, M., & Blanchard, K. (2003). *Business leadership. Jossey-Bass Business and Management Series.* San Francisco, CA: John Wiley & Sons.

Hesselbein, F., Goldsmith, M., & Beckhard, R. (1997). *The organization of the future.* San Francisco, CA: Jossey-Bass.

Higgs, M., & Rowland, D. (2005). All changes great and small: Exploring approaches to change and its leadership. *Journal of Change Management, 5*(2), 121–151. Retrieved October 12, 2010, from EBSCOhost.

Humphreys, J., & Einstein, W. (2004). Leadership and temperament congruence: Extending the expectancy model of work motivation. *Journal of Leadership & Organizational Studies, 10*(4), 58-80. Retrieved October 12, 2010, from Gale Powersearch database.

Igbaira, M. (2001). Virtual society: The driving forces and arrangements. *Journal of Information Technology Cases and Applications, 3*(2), 1-6. Retrieved October 22, 2010, from EBSCOhost.

Jacob, J. I., Bond, J. T., & Galinsky, E. (2008). Six critical ingredients in creating an effective workplace. *Psychologist-Manager Journal, 11*(1), 141-161. Retrieved October 14, 2010, from EBSCOhost.

Jones, C. (2004). The costs of nurse turnover. *Journal of Nursing Administration, 34,* 562-570. Retrieved November 22, 2010 from ProQuest health & medicine.

Jordan, M. (2005). Engage staff. *Charter, 76*(8), 46. Retrieved February 6, 2010, from EBSCOhost.

Kane, M.T. (2009) Validating the interpretations and uses of test scores. In: Lissitz R.W. (Ed.) *The Concept of Validity: Revisions, New Directions and Applications* (pp. 39-64). Charlotte, NC: Information Age Publishing, Inc.

Jung, D.I. & Sosik, J. J. (2002). Transformational leadership in work groups. The role of empowerment, cohesiveness, and collective-efficacy on perceived performance. *Small Group Research 33*(3), 313-336. doi: 10.1177/10496402033003002

Kahn, W. (1990). Psychological conditions of personal engagement and disengagement at work. *Academy of Management Journal, 33*(4), 692-724. Retrieved May 30, 2010, from EBSCOhost.

Kark, R., & Van Dijk, D. (2007). Motivation to lead, motivation to follow: The role of the self-regulatory focus in leadership processes. *Academy of Management Review, 32*(2), 500-528. Retrieved November 12, 2010 from EBSCOhost.

Kerfoot, K. (2008). Staff engagement: It starts with the leader. *Nursing Economics, 25. (1), 47-48.* Retrieved February 12, 2011, From ProQuest health and medicine.

Ketter, P. (2008). What's the big deal about employee engagement? *Training and Development, 62*(1), 45-49. Retrieved October 8, 2010, from ProQuest.

Khanna, S. (2008). Increasing employee retention through employee engagement – a challenge for HR. *Annual Handbook of Human Resource Initiatives,* 1-8. Retrieved October 24, 2010, from http://hrod.empi.in/images/Employeeengagement.pdf

Kirkpatrick, S., & Locke, E. (1996). Direct and indirect effects of three core charismatic leadership components on performance and attitude. *Journal of Applied Psychology, 81,* 36-51. Retrieved March 14, 2010, from EBSCOhost.

Klein, K., & Kozlowski, S. (2000). *Multilevel theory, research, and methods in organizations.* San Francisco, CA: Jossey Bass.

Kleinman, C. (2004). The relationship between managerial leadership behaviors and staff nurse retention. *Hospital Topics: Research and Perspectives on Healthcare, 82*(4), 2-9. Retrieved December 10, 2010, from EBSCOhost.

Klie, S. (2007). Senior leadership drives employee engagement: Study. *Canadian HR Reporter, 20*(20), 1-2. Retrieved September 17, 2010, from ProQuest.

Koh, K., & Witarsa, M. P. (2003). A review of data analysis for the behavioral sciences using SPSS. *Journal of Educational and Behavioral Statistics, 28*(1), 77-81. doi:10.3102/10769986028001077

Kouzes, J., & Posner, B. (2003). The five practices of exemplary leadership. In *Business leadership: Jossey-Bass business and management series.* San Francisco, CA: John Wiley & Sons.

Kreitner, R., & Kinicki, A. (2004). *Organizational behavior.* New York, NY: McGraw-Hill.

Lafer, G. (2005). Hospital speedups and the fiction of a nursing shortage. *Labor Studies Journal, 30*(1), 27-46. Retrieved November 22, 2010, from EBSCOhost.

Leedy, P. D., & Orrmrod, (2010). *Practical research: Planning & design.* Upper Saddle River, NJ: Pearson.

Lewin, K., & Lippitt, R. (1938). An experimental approach to the study of autocracy and democracy: A preliminary note. *Sociometry, 1,* 292-300. Retrieved October16, 2010, from EBSCOhost.

Little, B., & Little, P. (2006). Employee engagement: Conceptual issues. *Journal of   Organizational Culture Communications and Conflict, 10*(1), 111-121. Retrieved October 24, 2010, from Gale Power Search.

Locke, E. A. (1976). The nature and causes of job satisfaction. In M. D. Dunnette (Ed.), *Handbook of industrial and organizational psychology* (pp. 1297–1349). Palo Alto, CA: Consulting Psychologists Press.

Lowe, K. B., Kroeck, K. G., & Sivasubramaniam, N. (1996). Effectiveness correlates of transformational and transactional leadership: A meta-analytic.

Leadership Quarterly, 7(3), 385-425. doi:
10.1016/S1048-9843(96)90027-2

Macey, W. H., & Schneider, B. (2008a). Engaged in
engagement: We are delighted we did it. *Industrial
& Organizational Psychology, 1*(1), 76-83. Retrieved
November 24, 2010, from EBSCOHost.

Macey, W. H., & Schneider, B. (2008b). The meaning of
employee engagement. *Industrial and Organizational
Psychology, 1*(1), 3-30. Retrieved November 24,
2010, from EBSCOhost.

Manthey, M. (2007). Nurse manager as culture builder.
Nurse Leader, 5(4), 54-56. Retrieved   May 16, 2010
from ProQuest health and medicine.

McGregor, D. M. (1960). *The human side of enterprise.* New
York, NY: McGraw Hill.

McGuire E., & Kennerly, S. (2006). Nurse managers as
transformational and transactional leaders. *Nursing
Economics, 24*(4), 179-185. Retrieved March 30,
2010 from EBSCOhost.

Mettler, M., & Kemper, D. (2007). A healthwise gray
paper: How the baby boomers can save health
care. *Healthwise White Paper Series, 1-6.* Retrieved

March 14, 2009, from
www.healthwise.org/dissertation_nursing.

Moon, F. C., Luk, A. L., Sok, M. L., Siu, M. Y., & Iat,
K.V. (2008). Factors influencing Macao nurses'
intention to leave employment. *Journal of Clinical
Nursing,* 18(6), 893-901. Retrieved February 6, from
EBSCOhost.

Morrison, E. E., Burke, G. C., & Greene, L. (2007).
Meaning in motivation: does your organization
need an inner life? *Journal of Health & Human
Services Administration, 30*(1), 98-115. Retrieved
February 6, 2010, from EBSCOhost.

Mosadeghrad, A. M., Ferlie, E., & Rosenberg, D. (2008).
A study of the relationship between job
satisfaction, organizational commitment and
turnover intention among hospital employees.
Health Services Management Research, 21, 211–227.
Retrieved from EBSCOhost.

Nahavandi, A. (2003). *The art and science of leadership.*
Upper Saddle River NJ: Prentice Hall.

Neuman, W. L. (2003). *Social research methods* (5th ed.).
Upper Saddle River, NJ: Prentice Hall.

Neuman, W. L. (2006). *Social research methods: qualitative and quantitative approaches.* Upper Saddle River, NJ: Prentice Hall.

Newcomb, K. (2005). Transformational leadership: Four keys to help you and your Organization stay focused on continuous improvement and greater value. *Debt Cubed, 20*(6), 34-36. Retrieved November 22, 2010, from EBSCOhost.

Nutall, P., Shankar, A., Beverland, M. B., Hooper, C. S (2011). Mapping the unarticulated Potential of Qualitative Research: Stepping out from the Shadow of Quantitative Studies. *Journal of advertising research,* 51, 153-163. Retrieved July 1, 2011 from EBSCOhost.

Paradise, A. (2008). Influences engagement. *Training and Development, 62*(1), 54-60. Retrieved October 24, 2010, from ProQuest.

Piersol, B. (2007). Employee engagement and power to the edge. *Performance Improvement, 46*(4), 30-33. Retrieved November 24, 2010, from ProQuest.

Rajapaksa, S. & Rothstein, W. (2009). Factors that influence decisions of men and women to leave nursing. *Nursing`Forum, 44*, 195 – 107. Retrieved February 12, 2010, from ProQuest.

Ribelin, P. J. (2003). Retention reflects leadership style. *Nursing Management, 34*(8), 18-20. Retrieved November 20, 2010 from EBSCOhost.

Rumrill, P. D. (2004). Speaking of research. Non-manipulation quantitative designs. *Work, 22*(3), 255-260. Retrieved May 1, 2011 from EBSCOhost.

Saks, A. (2006). Antecedents and consequences of employee engagement. *Journal of Managerial Psychology, 21*(7), 600-615. Retrieved April 9, 2008, from ProQuest.

Salanova, M., Lorente, L., Chambel, M. J., & Martínez, I. M. (2011). Linking transformational leadership to nurses' extra-role performance: the mediating role of self-efficacy and work engagement. *Journal Of Advanced Nursing, 67*(10), 2256-2266. Retrieved on June 6, 2014 from EbscoHost.doi:10.1111/j.1365-2648.2011.05652.x

Salkind, N. J. (2003). *Exploring research*. Upper Saddle River, NJ: Prentice Hall.

Salkind, N. J. (2006). *Exploring research*. Upper Saddle River, NJ: Pearson Education.

Schaufeli, W.B., & Salanova, M. (2007). Work engagement: An emerging psychological concept and its implications for organizations. In S.W. Gilliland, D.D. Steiner, & D.P.Skarlicki (Eds.), Research in social issues in management: Managing social and ethical issues in organizations. Greenwich, CT: Information Age Publishers.

Schaufeli, W., & Bakker, A. (2003). *Utrecht work engagement scale (UWES). Preliminary manual version 1.* Occupational health psychology unit, University of Utrecht. Retrieved January 3, 2010 from UWES_engagescale.pdf – Adobe Reader

Schaufeli, W, B., Bakker, A. B. & Salanova, M. (2006). The measurement of work engagement with a short questionnaire. *Educational and psychological measurement, 66*(4), 701-716. Retrieved September 24 2010, from Google.

Schein, E. (1992). *Organizational culture and leadership.* San Francisco, CA: Jossey-Bass.

Schleicher, D. J., Watt, J. D., & Greguras, G. J. (2004). Re-examining the job-satisfaction performance relationship: The complexity of attitudes. *Journal of*

Applied Psychology, 89, 165–177. Retrieved November 24, 2010, from EBSCOhost.

Scott, R. (1990). Symbols and organizations: From Barnhard to the institutionalists. In O. Williamson (Ed.). *Organizational theory.* New York, NY: Oxford University Press.

Scott, J. (2013). How healthcare leaders can increase emotional intelligence. Radiology Management, 11-16.

Seijts, G., & Crim, D. (2006). What engages employees the most or, the ten c's of employee engagement. *Ivey Business Journal Online,* 1-5. Retrieved April 26, 2010, from ProQuest.

Simon, K. (2011). Dissertation and scholarly research: Recipes for success. Seattle, WA. Dissertation Success, LLC. Retrieved January 28, 2012 from www.dissertationrecipes.com

Simpson M.R. (2009) Engagement at work: a review of the literature. International Journal of Stevens, J. P. (2009). *Applied multivariate statistics for the social sciences* (5th ed.). Mahwah, NJ: Routledge Academic.

Nursing Studies 46, 1012 –1024. Retrieved on June 6, 2014 from Google scholar

Song, J., Kolb, J. A., Lee, U., & Kim, H. (2012). Role of Transformational Leadership in Effective Organizational Knowledge Creation Practices: Mediating Effects of Employees' Work Engagement. *Human Resource Development Quarterly, 23(*1), 65-101. Retrieved on June 6, 2014 from EbscoHost.

Spetz, J. (2005). Public policy and nurse staffing. *Journal of Nursing Administration, 35*(1), 14–16. Retrieved March 30, 2009 from ProQuest health & medicine.

Steinberg, W. J. (2008). *Statistics Alive!* Thousand Oaks, CA: Sage Publications.

Sugrue, N. M. (2005). Public policy initiatives and the nursing shortage. *Journal of Nursing Administration, 35*(1), 19–22. Retrieved March 16, 2009 from ProQuest health & medicine.

Syndell, M. A. (2008). The role of emotional intelligence in transformational leadership style. *Capella University.* Retrieved May 3, 2014, from the ProQuest Dissertations and Theses database.

Tabachnick, B. G. & Fidell, L. S. (2012). *Using multivariate statistics* (6th ed.). Boston, MA: Pearson.

Takase, M., Yamashita, N., & Oba, K. (2008). Nurses' leaving intentions: Antecedents and mediating factors. *Journal of Advanced Nursing, 62*(3), 295-306. Retrieved February 11, 2011. EBSCOhost

The Gallup Organization. (2005). *Employee engagement: The employee side of the human sigma equation.* Retrieved February 20, 2010, from http:www.gallup.com

Towers, P. HR Services (2003). Working today: *Understanding what drives employee engagement.* Retrieved October 26, 2010, from Google.

Upenieks, V. (2003). What constitutes effective leadership? Perceptions of magnet and Non magnet nurse leaders. *Journal of Nursing Administration,* 33, 456-467. Retrieved November 10, 2010 from EBSCOhost.

Upenieks, V. (2005). Recruitment and retention strategies: A magnet hospital prevention model. *MEDSURG Nursing, 14,* 21-27. Retrieved November 10, 2010, from EBSCOhost.

U.S. Department of Labor. (2007). *Occupations with largest job growth.* Retrieved April 16, 2010 from http://www.bls.gov/emp/emptab3.htm

U.S. Department of Health and Human Services; Health Resources and Services Administration, Bureau of Health Professions. (2004a). *What is behind HRSA'S projected supply, demand, and shortage of registered nurses?* Retrieved April12, 2010, from http://bhpr.hrsa.gov/healthworkforce/reports/ behindrnprojections/2.htm

U.S. Department of Health and Human Services; Health Resources and Services Administration, Bureau of Health Professions. (2004b). *What is behind HRSA'S projected supply, demand, and shortage of registered nurses?* Retrieved January 7, 2007, from http://bhpr.hrsa.gov/healthworkforce/reports/ behindrnprojections/2.htm

Varnhagen, C. K., Gushta, M., Daniels, J., Peters, T. C., Parmar, N., Law, D., Hirsch R., Takach, B. S., & Johnson, T. (2005). How informed is online informed consent? *Ethics & Behavior, 15*(1), 37-48. doi: 10.1207/s15327019eb1501_3

Vilma Z, Egle K (2007) Improving motivation among health care workers in private health care organisations: a perspective of nursing personnel. Baltic Journal of Management. 2, 2, 213-224.

Vroom, V. H., & Jago, A. G. (2007). The role of the situation in leadership. *American Psychologist, 62*(1), 17-24. Retrieved March 29, 2010, from EBSCOhost.

Wagner, S. E. (2006). Staff retention from "satisfied" to "engaged." *Nursing Management, 37*(3), 24-30. Retrieved February 6, 2010, from EBSCOhost.

Walumbwa, F. O., Avolio, B. J., Zhu, W. (2008). How Transformational leadership weaves its influence on individual job performance: The role of identification and efficacy beliefs. Personal Psychology, *61*(4), 793-825. Retrieved March 3, 2011 from   EBSCOhost.

Walumbwa, F. O., Lawler, J. J., & Avolio, B. J. (2007). Leadership, individual differences, And work-related attitudes: A cross-culture investigation. Applied Psychology: An international review, *56*(2), 212-230. Retrieved March 12, 2011 from EBSCOhost.

Welbourne, T. M. (2007). Employee engagement: Beyond the fad and into the executive suite. *Leader to Leader, 2007*(44), 45-51. Retrieved March 10, 2011, from ProQuest.

Wenzel, H. (1994). Post-industrial lives: Roles and relationships in the 21st century. *The American Journal of Sociology, 99*(5), 1370-1372. Retrieved November 21, 2011, from EBSCOhost.

Whetstone, J. T. (2002). Personalism and moral leadership: The servant leader with a transforming vision. *Business Ethics: A European Review, 11*(4), 385-392. Retrieved May 23, 2010, from EBSCOhost.

Whiteley, P. (2006). History repeating itself. *Personnel Today,* 28-30. Retrieved October 16, 2010, from EBSCOhost.

White, B. (2008). *The state of employee engagement 2008.* Retrieved November 16, 2010, from http://www.blessingwhite.com/EEE__report.asp

Wildermuth, C., & Wildermuth, M. (2008). Employee involvement, corporate culture, job satisfaction, personality traits, leadership, work life balance.

Training and Development, 62(1), 54-60. Retrieved November 21, 2011 from ProQuest.

Wren, J. T. (1995). *The leader's companion: Insights on leadership through the ages.* New York, NY: The Free Press.

Yukl, G. A. (2006). *Leadership in organizations.* Upper Saddle River, NJ: Prentice Hall.

Zbierajewski, J., Kachmarik, V., & O'Dell, S. (2007). Bridging the faculty shortage gap. *Nursing Management, 38*(7), 8. Retrieved October 10 2010, from EBSCOhost.

www.ingramcontent.com/pod-product-compliance
Lightning Source LLC
Chambersburg PA
CBHW071330210326
41597CB00015B/1396